Wow! This is not your father's church budgeti
biblical and theological with shading of good hist
is crisp. The chapters, and even subpoints and ot
able to be used as standalones. A businessman wit
heart. This book is a gift.

MARK DEVER, senior pastor, Capitol Hill Baptist Church (Washington, DC)

Almost every church has a budget. And yet too many churches give little thought to the spiritual dimensions of planning, developing, and communicating a budget. That's what Jamie means to remedy in this immensely helpful book. While my Presbyterian sensibilities may quibble here or there, I'm grateful for a terrific resource that is so biblical, practical, accessible, and wise. This is a book we've needed for a long time.

KEVIN DEYOUNG, senior pastor, Christ Covenant Church (Matthews, NC); assistant professor of systematic theology, RTS Charlotte

If I had just one physical item to evaluate the heartbeat of a local church, it would not be attendance records, baptismal reports, committee assignments, or staff alignments. I would ask to see the church budget. The budget of the church is what reveals where the church's heart is in the midst of a myriad of ministries and missions.

Jamie Dunlop has done the local church a great service in this new volume, *Budgeting for a Healthy Church.* This is not a book about "budgeting." It is a book about values—my values, your values—and, as stewards of the ministries of the local church, it is about the church's values. Nor is this book simply another theoretical treatise. These principles have been beaten out on the anvil of personal experience in one of the most biblically-minded local congregations in America.

Money talks. And it speaks volumes about what we truly believe is important and of high priority. Get this book before you plan your next budget. Read it . . . and reap!

O. S. HAWKINS, president/CEO, GuideStone Financial Resources; former pastor, First Baptist Church in Dallas

Jamie's work on this book illustrates his practical, biblical approach to addressing the hardest part of the job for most pastors. His wisdom will help you know how to integrate your budget into the biblical mandate for the church.

DALE SUTHERLAND, lead pastor, McLean Bible Church (Virginia)

Many pastors' eyes glaze over, or (alternatively) their hearts are struck with terror, when they hear the word "budgeting." Some of us just aren't "numbers guys," and beyond wanting to make sure that our fellow church staff are taken care of and the mission of the church is suitably funded, we don't have a big picture on church budgeting that looks theologically at the issue, nor a grasp of the details that go into working that out practically. Jamie Dunlop does. And you are holding it. Pastors, read it. And get it to your elders and deacons too, and members. Oh, that we would all have a more biblical and practical vision of how to go about this necessary aspect of life together in a congregation, and especially that we would see how our theology of ministry ought to work its way out in the church's budget.

LIGON DUNCAN, chancellor and CEO, Reformed Theological Seminary

This book offers sound financial stewardship suggestions and more importantly, presents every suggestion in the context of faithfulness to Scripture. It is more than a budgeting book; it will challenge you to reflect on how your church uses its resources in light of biblical truth. The book is concise, well-written, and easy to read. If you are a pastor/elder deciding how to best oversee the ministry of the church, a deacon (as I am) with financial administration responsibilities, or simply a member of the congregation who wants to pray more specifically for your church leaders as they shepherd those entrusted to them, this book has much to offer.

RHEA D. THORNTON, chief risk officer, Fannie Mae Multifamily Mortgage (retired); treasurer, Immanuel Church (Nashville, TN)

Your church budget says a lot about your church; it also says a lot about your God! Jamie Dunlop has again served local churches well by not only giving practical wisdom to budgeting but by showing how the budget can be used pastorally to grow the spiritual health of the church. If you're a pastor or work with your church's budget, invest in this book—buy it, read it, and invest in helping your church be financially faithful.

STEVE BOYER, controller, The Salvation Army USA

Jamie Dunlop shows us what is interesting in the subject of church budgets—starting with his argument that how a church spends its money "reveals its heart, its values, and its priorities." Recognizing that while God doesn't need our money to accomplish his purposes, Dunlop does accurately argue that a church budget is part of the obedience and faithfulness responsibility of any church. This book is a good guide for any serious pastor, elder, church administrator, or congregant desiring to understand the principles, prayer attitudes, and practical realities of a church budget while experiencing the joy of stewardship along the way.

BOB DOLL, chief equity strategist, Nuveen

Jamie Dunlop masterfully weaves together his business mind and his pastor's heart. It's a book I wish I had read twenty-five years ago. Filled with biblical principles, financial insight, and practical helps, *Budgeting for a Healthy Church* is a resource that every pastor and church leader should read!

DENNIS BLYTHE, executive pastor, The Church at Brook Hills (Birmingham, AL)

BUDGETING FOR A HEALTHY CHURCH

BUDGETING FOR A HEALTHY CHURCH

ALIGNING FINANCES
WITH BIBLICAL PRIORITIES
FOR MINISTRY

JAMIE DUNLOP

 ZONDERVAN®  9Marks

ZONDERVAN

Budgeting for a Healthy Church
Copyright © 2019 by James Dunlop

ISBN 978-0-310-09386-2 (softcover)

ISBN 978-0-310-09387-9 (ebook)

Requests for information should be addressed to:
Zondervan, *3900 Sparks Dr. SE, Grand Rapids, Michigan 49546*

Art direction: Rick Scuezs Design
Interior design: Kait Lamphere

Printed in the United States of America

HB 04.30.2024

CONTENTS

FOREWORD

Have you ever wondered why books like this one have a foreword? Why would one author ask another to write a minichapter at the front of his book? I think the reason is twofold. First, it's meant to give you, the reader, confidence in the author of the book, to assure you he is qualified to write about his subject. Second, it's to give you a sense of whether this book is one you'd benefit from.

So here's the first question: *Are you in good hands as you read this book?* I'm glad to say that you are! Jamie Dunlop had a successful career in the world of business and was then called by his church to serve as an associate pastor. For the past ten years he has helped pastor the members of Capitol Hill Baptist Church in Washington, DC, while giving particular oversight to matters related to administration and finance. He has also been involved in 9Marks, a ministry committed to creating resources that help foster healthy churches. Much of what is released under the banner of the ministry is produced by the church. This means it has been field-tested and shown to be effective. What you read in this book is not abstract, but practical and proven.

Here's the second question: *Should you read this book?* That depends on who you are. 9Marks exists to help unhealthy churches become healthy and healthy churches to remain that way. What we know to be true about our use of money personally is equally true about our use of money congregationally—it can demonstrate spiritual health or spiritual weakness. If you are a member of a church, this book will help you better understand how your church can budget its money toward health. If you are a pastor or leader of a church or otherwise involved in preparing and monitoring that budget, it will prove especially beneficial. It may not tell you how much to allocate to each column on a spreadsheet, but it will give you biblical wisdom on how money is so closely tied to our God-given mission. It won't answer your every "how" question, but it will certainly assist you to better understand the many "what" questions about your church and its finances.

What Jamie wants you to know is this: your budget reveals your values. The way your church allocates its financial resources tells so much about what you value most and about what you mean to accomplish in the name of Jesus Christ. With time short and the mission urgent, there's every reason to ensure that your church and its budget are healthy.

Tim Challies

ACKNOWLEDGMENTS

As you might imagine, I have many to thank for their partnership in this project. My wife, Joan, and several friends in ministry—Dennis Blythe, Trent Hunter, David Parker, Lindsey Parker, Gustav Pritchard, Jon Rourke, Brad Thayer, Cody Volkers, Sebastian Traeger, Lincoln VerMeer, and Annie Collins—all read through the manuscript and provided critical feedback. Jonathan Leeman at 9Marks Ministries helped shape these ideas and worked to turn them into a finished product. Finally, the congregation of Capitol Hill Baptist Church, where I serve as a pastor, generously gave me time to write because they love the wider church of Jesus Christ.

SERIES PREFACE

9Marks exists to equip church leaders with a biblical vision and practical resources for displaying God's glory to the nations through healthy churches.

As such, the 9Marks series of books is premised on two basic ideas. First, the local church is far more important to the Christian life than many Christians today realize. Second, local churches grow in life and vitality as they organize their lives around God's Word. God speaks. Churches should listen and follow. It's that simple. When a church listens and follows, it begins to look like the One it is following. It reflects his love and holiness. It displays his glory. A church will look like him as it listens to him.

Out of these ideas comes the 9Marks series of books. Some target pastors. Some target church members. Hopefully all will combine careful biblical examination, theological reflection, cultural consideration, corporate application, and even a bit of individual exhortation. The best Christian books are both theological and practical.

It's our prayer that God will use this book and the others in the series to help prepare his bride, the church, with radiance and splendor for the day of his coming.

To access 9Marks's free resources for building healthy churches, visit www.9marks.org.

INTRODUCTION

Where your treasure is, there your heart will be also.

Matthew 6:21

Jesus's observation in Matthew 6:21 was about individuals, but it's also true of churches. To understand what really matters to a church, look past its vision statement, past its website, past its glossy brochures, and look at its budget. Follow the money. What a church treasures—how it spends money—reveals its heart, its values, and its priorities.

This truth is what breathes life into the otherwise tedious topic of church budgeting and finances. A church budget is more than spreadsheets and numbers. It's a window into the heart of a church, illuminating the values and priorities of God's people. If you care about your church, you will care about its budget because a budget reveals, facilitates, and sometimes calcifies how a church does its work. That's what this book is all about.

The goal of digging into the otherwise mundane topic of budgeting is to ask a simple question: *Is your budget helping or hurting the health of your church?* That is, do the priorities expressed in the budget reflect biblical priorities? Do they align with God's purposes for your church? And what kind of ministry are they shaping?

The Burden of This Book

"Most books," one author wrote, "have their origin in some kind of enduring mental distraction that has grown so large and ungainly

15

in the author's mind that only hammering it out at book length will fully exorcise the thing."[1] True enough! I can certainly relate because that's been my experience in writing this book. It has grown out of a persistent burden I've had that church leaders, pastors, and those responsible for the financial health of the church should understand the true nature of the church budget: *a church budget is a spiritual tool with spiritual aims.* A church budget has spiritual value when we get it right and does spiritual harm when we get it wrong. As a result, seeing a church's budget merely, or even primarily, as a financial tool grossly underestimates what it is.

A wealthy gentleman asked my church's senior pastor to lunch shortly after he began his ministry. He began the meeting with an intriguing proposition.

"I'll make the same deal with you as I did with the previous pastors: you take care of the preaching; I'll take care of the budget."

His offer was a generous one. By proposing to "take care of the budget" he did not merely mean "I'll control the budget" but also "I'll give what's needed to balance the budget." In a struggling church, that proposal was a financial lifeline. But appropriately, the pastor declined: "Thank you, but no thank you." You cannot call preaching "spiritual" and the budget merely "financial."

It's all spiritual.

How about you? Do you operate with a spiritual/financial dichotomy in your mind? Let's start with a few diagnostic questions.

- Who talks about the budget with the congregation? Pastors? Elders? Deacons? A finance team? Do they have spiritual objectives in mind during those discussions?
- What is the budget trying to accomplish? How well do those priorities align with God's mission for the church as revealed in the Bible?

---

1. Mary Eberstadt, *How the West Really Lost God: A New Theory of Secularization* (West Conshohocken, PA: Templeton, 2013), 3.

- To what extent does the church's handling of money teach the congregation how to be faithful stewards of their own money?

These are just a few initial questions to get started. But here's the point: seeing the budget as a spiritual document and not "just" a financial document will *significantly* change the answers to all these questions.

I've designed this book to assist you in using the church budget as a spiritual tool. I intend to help you in three specific ways.

First, I hope to show you how a church's budget reveals its true philosophy of ministry. A philosophy of ministry—the guiding principles that determine a church's priorities and decisions—is tightly tethered to its budget. You cannot protect or change your philosophy of ministry unless you understand the budget's role in shaping it.

Second, we'll look at how to evaluate a budget against the standard of Scripture. Very often, we assume the Bible has little to say about the infrastructure of churches, but a closer look reveals a wealth of wisdom that's often ignored.

Finally, I want to teach you how to use the budget as a potent tool for pastoral ministry. For too many pastors, the budget is a missed opportunity.

What's in This Book?

Hopefully you're beginning to see that this book is quite different from most church budgeting books you may have read (if, like me, you're into that sort of thing). Most books on church budgeting are about *how* to do budgeting, and the principles they teach apply equally well across a wide range of Christian denominations and even to other religious groups and secular nonprofits. This book is less about the budget process and more about the budget itself—what it says about your heart, priorities, and values. It's not a *how* book but a *what* book. *What* ministry is the budget funding? *What* impact does that have on the congregation? And *what* does the Bible say about those priorities?

The book begins by asking what God's goal is for a church's budget. Based on that answer, in chapter two we look at financial leadership in a church. Pastors cannot delegate all responsibility for the budget to others, as if finances are somehow separate from the ministry of the church. Then, this being a *what* book, the chapters that follow move from one section of the budget to the next—from the income line to staff to programs to outreach to administration and facilities—and examine what Scripture says about each of these areas. Finally, we'll close with a chapter on the budget as a pastoral tool for teaching.

Throughout the book, you'll find various worksheets and checklists I've created to help put principles into practice. You will most certainly need to customize these if you're going to use them. As such, you'll find editable copies of these at https://www.9marks.org/budgetresources. A quick caveat about these resources: if some of these principles are already baked into your thinking, you'll probably find some of the worksheets redundant and unnecessary. On the other hand, if you or your leadership team is not used to operating with the principles suggested in the book, these worksheets and checklists may be useful while you get used to new ways of thinking.

Who Wrote This?

It will help to know a little about me as you get into these chapters. This book is written by a pastor—a pastor with a shepherd's heart and a businessman's head. I began attending my church as a business professional working in consulting and private equity with a plan to stay in Washington, DC, "a few" years before moving away for school. I fell in love with my church, however, and after ten years in business, I left my job to serve them as a pastor, which has now been my privilege for the last decade. This means that as you read through these pages, you'll likely see my respect for the tools of business combined with my love for the local church and a keen desire to serve well as a faithful undershepherd of Jesus Christ.

Whom Is This Book For?

Since this is a *what* book instead of a *how* book, I've written with two main audiences in mind. First, I'm writing for those who are ministers of the Word: pastors, elders—or future pastors and elders—who are responsible for teaching God's Word to God's people. I want to broaden your understanding of budgets and finances by showing you how relevant they are for your ministry and how you can use them well to serve and equip God's people. Second, I'm writing for those who work directly with church budgets: church administrators, deacons, finance committees, and so forth. If you're in this second category, I want to let you know up front that I believe your work is essential, but it must be closely connected to the pastoral leadership of your church. Very little in this book can be put into practice without the support of your pastors. So if your pastor just handed you this book because you're "the budget person," you have my permission to hand it back and insist that you will only read it if he does as well.

No matter who you are, I hope you will read this book with an awareness that we must all give a future accounting to God. "Nothing in all creation is hidden from God's sight. Everything is uncovered and laid bare before the eyes of him to whom we must give account" (Heb. 4:13). Budgeting is not ultimately about following the right rules. It's about right stewardship. We are all stewards as individuals—of our money, our time, our relationships, our skills—and as those involved in church budgeting, we bear a special additional responsibility to steward the resources contributed by God's people. My prayer is that this little book will help you do that better, for the eternal good of your congregation and to the everlasting glory of our great God and Savior, Jesus Christ.

CHAPTER ONE

WHY DOES GOD CARE ABOUT YOUR CHURCH BUDGET?

This is not a book about money.

It is indeed a book about church budgets, so you'd be forgiven for thinking it's a book about money. But it's not. It's a book about value. Ultimately, it's a book about the value of Jesus Christ. It's about how his extraordinary kindness, mercy, justice, beauty, goodness, and power have captivated and transformed our hearts through his death and resurrection so that we spend our lives proclaiming who he is. That lifelong proclamation involves what we do with our money and, consequentially, what our churches do with their money. So while your church budget is written in the language of money, it's not ultimately about the money. It's about the glory of our Savior.

And that's the main reason a church's budget is important: *it should reveal what the congregation truly values.* That means every budget tells a story. A good budget will tell a story about Jesus and his promises being worth more than anything this world could offer. What story does your church's budget tell?

The Right Goal Is Critical

In order to get a church budget that tells the right story, you need to begin with the right goal. So that's where we'll begin this book.

Take this situation as an example: First Church's budget committee is debating how much money to allocate to its children's ministry. The children's minister, Nate, is proposing a huge increase in funding to turn his wing of the building into a first-rate children's attraction. "Think of how many visitors this will draw!"

But some on the committee aren't sold on the idea of spending money this way. "What are we attracting them with?" they ask. "Jesus or the thrills of a theme park?"

Nate responds, "What does it matter? What matters is that we get them in the door. We're buying an opportunity to tell them the gospel!"

Here we see the clash of competing ministry philosophies. Nate wants to fund the Great Commission. Others fear his planned renovations will just fund more church consumerism.

Do you see how often budget conversations are actually ministry conversations? And we immediately want to ask, who's right? Nate or the skeptics? The answer to that question will depend on the church's goal for its budget.

So what's your church's goal for its budget? Or even better, let's rewrite that question to reflect the opinion that matters most. What is *God's* goal for your church's budget? Is that goal captured in your vision statement? Perhaps it's something like: "We exist that First Church might spread everywhere the fragrance of the knowledge of Christ (2 Cor. 2:14)." Or maybe your goal is more specific, like "we want to save for our minister's retirement" or "we want to start a new church across town" or "we want to fund a missionary to the Pashtuns of Afghanistan."

God Doesn't Need Your Budget

Articulating God's goal for your church's budget is surprisingly challenging because God doesn't need your budget. Psalm 50:12 makes this clear: "If I were hungry I would not tell you, for the world is mine, and all that is in it." God isn't waiting with his hands tied, helplessly hoping against hope that you'll lend him a hand. "My purpose will stand, and I will do all that I please" (Isa. 46:10). God's plans are not mere hopes, dreams, or ambitions. They are inexorable facts that *will* come to pass. God "works out everything in conformity with the purpose of his will" (Eph. 1:11)—regardless of what you do with your budget. "Our God is in heaven; he does whatever pleases him" (Ps. 115:3). Understand that God doesn't need your budget.

But this doesn't mean your budget and what you do with God's money are unimportant to him. They're just important to him for different reasons than you may have thought. And getting your budget right begins with understanding why God cares about it.

You may be reading this book because you aren't satisfied with your church budget. Maybe the process is painful (as it is in so many churches) or you've sensed that your financial decisions are disconnected from the ministry of the church. Maybe you're concerned that your budget doesn't inspire people (again, a common problem). Perhaps you find budgeting to be confusing and arbitrary, or your church's giving is lacking or declining. Often these problems stem from a budget that's oriented toward the wrong goal. You may have had good things in mind, but maybe not the things God has in mind.

I can't promise to fix all your budgetary problems, but I have great confidence that reorienting your budget toward the right goal can alleviate many of the challenges I just described—or at least change how you perceive them. My hope is that as your church aligns its budget to its God-given goals, it will invest its money more wisely and your whole congregation will better reflect the goodness of God—to the glory of God.

God's Goal for Your Church's Money

A helpful way of understanding God's goal for your church's budget is found in Jesus's parable of the talents in Matthew 25. In this section of Matthew, Jesus explains in a series of stories how kingdom citizens should live in light of the coming consummation of the kingdom. In the parable, a wealthy master (who represents God) goes away on a long journey and entrusts large sums of money (talents) to three of his servants (who represent us). He gives five talents to one servant, two to another, one to a third—"each according to his ability" (v. 15). When the master returns, he calls them to account. The servant with five talents has made five more, and the master commends him: "Well done, good and faithful servant. You have been faithful over a little; I will set you over much. Enter into the joy of your master" (v. 21 ESV).

The second servant has also doubled his money, and he receives the same commendation. Then we get to the third servant. Believing his master to be a "hard man," he hid his talent in the ground and now gives it back. But if he expected grudging thanks when he returned the money, he is tragically mistaken. "His master replied, 'You wicked and slothful servant! . . . take the talent from him and give it to him who has the ten. . . . And cast the worthless servant into the outer darkness. In that place there will be weeping and gnashing of teeth'" (vv. 26, 28, 30 ESV).

Like many of Jesus's parables, this one has a twist at the end. Without that twist, the parable seems almost moralistic: "Do your best, and if you work hard for God, he'll be pleased with you." Yet that reading is precisely upside down. After all, the first servant received the same commendation as the second, even though he accomplished twice as much.

The twist is what happens to the third servant. At the end of the parable, the master sends him to hell. Did you catch that? "In that place there will be weeping and gnashing of teeth."

Really? He didn't lose the talent, did he? He gave it back! Hell? Just because he didn't return more than he was given? That doesn't sound fair at all. What's going on here?

The key that unlocks this parable is what the third servant's actions communicate about his real master. The third servant attempted to serve not one master but two. He thought he'd be fine if the master returned because he'd still have the money. And he'd be fine if the master didn't return because he'd spent the time working for himself. In other words, he was hedging his bets *because he didn't have faith in the master*. He may have doubted that the master would return, or he may have doubted that the master was worthy of his work while he was away.

But any doubt about this master is seen, in the end, to be ridiculous. After all, the master represents God. So when the third servant says, "I knew you to be a hard man," he reveals that he doesn't know his master at all. His choices show that his faith was only in himself, and his actions and words only defame the excellence of the master.

Contrast this with the actions of the first two servants. They believed that risking everything for the master was the best thing they could do for themselves. And they were right. Don't miss how their reward is described: "Enter into the joy of your master" (Matt. 25:21 ESV). Having gambled everything on the goodness of the master, their reward is to enjoy forever the goodness of the master.

This twist at the end shows that this is a parable about *faith*. As Jesus said in the Sermon on the Mount, no one can serve two masters. You can't have it both ways—living for yourself and living for God just enough to slip into heaven. The third servant is double-minded. As we discover, his life didn't evidence a weak faith; it evidenced that he had *no* faith.

James tells us that even the demons believe in God—and shudder (James 2:19). What's the difference between demonic faith and saving faith? Saving faith doesn't simply believe facts about God. It believes that God is good for us and that his rewards are worth having. Faith that pleases God is faith that believes "that he *rewards* those who earnestly seek him" (Heb. 11:6, emphasis mine). Saving faith believes that God is so good that we can joyfully venture everything on his promises.

When we do that, our lives become living advertisements of how good and desirable God is. However, when someone says, "I want to get into heaven, but I also want to hedge my bets because I don't really trust God's plans for me," then their life becomes a living advertisement that God is not good, that God is not trustworthy. They become like the faithless servant.

The fact that faith takes center stage in this parable doesn't demean the faithful servants' productivity or suggest that it didn't please their master. Instead, it shows us that their productivity wasn't ultimate. The master rejoiced in their work not for its own sake but because it revealed the servants' faith that he was worthy.

Consider again how the master described the first two servants: faithful. In faith-filled obedience, they bet with their lives that the master was worth their all, and so their lives testified to his goodness and glory. Faithfulness is God's goal for you as well. It's his goal for the stewardship of your time, your relationships, your talents (the word derives its modern meaning from this parable), and yes—your church budget.

What Is Faithfulness?

God's goal for every stewardship he's given you—including your church budget—is that you be found faithful. Let's pause for a moment then and unpack the concept of faithfulness that we find in Matthew 25. It includes two components.

First, it means we are *obedient*. Sometimes, even as Christians, we operate as if we can go about God's work any way we want, so long as we achieve good results for him. But that's not what Jesus teaches. We're not chess masters; we're the chess pieces. Accomplishing "great things" for God by following your own rules isn't faithful. To the contrary, it's a declaration that God's ways are not worth following, and it profanes the one you supposedly serve.

Second, faithfulness involves *risk*. When the path to follow Jesus and the path of this world run along in parallel, obedience doesn't testify much to the worth and value of Jesus Christ. But when obedience means risking what this world loves, it becomes a bold statement about the goodness and trustworthiness of the Master. How different this is from churches that equate being a good steward with being miserly!

Risk-taking obedience reveals the goodness and glory of God, which is what matters most in God's economy. That means your actions are valuable for much more than what they accomplish; they're valuable because of what they proclaim about God. His glory is paramount. For example, let's say you're deciding whether to go on a nice vacation or give your money to your church. You consider God's promise that treasure in heaven can never be destroyed (Matt. 6:20) and give the money to your church. Why does that please God? Not because he needs your money (though he may do great things with it). Instead, he delights in your generosity because it shows that you believe his Word. Or perhaps you take the vacation instead, reveling in the overwhelming goodness of God as you enjoy his good gifts (1 Tim. 4:4–5). Either way, the faith behind your actions matters because of the statement it makes about God.

Not every use of the word *faithful* in the Bible is best summarized as risk-taking obedience. Sometimes faithful simply means "loyal" or "trustworthy." But the concept of faithfulness in Matthew 25 is rich with significance, and it points to God's goal for your church budget.

How Can a Budget Be Faithful?

Let me flesh out how this concept applies to church budgeting. Very often, we act as if the goal of a church budget lies in what it can accomplish. If someone were to ask, "Why are we giving all this money?" you might point to the list of items in the budget. "People give money to pay the pastor, build the playground, save those children, start that church." But that accomplishment-focused mentality doesn't square with the fact that God is not wanting for money, and his purposes are much bigger than merely what your church's budget can accomplish. His purpose for your church's budget is that in your church's faithfulness—that is, in your risk-taking obedience—you show off and reveal how amazing he is. That's a tall order, I realize. But a church budget can do this in at least three ways:

1. As we give money to the church, our faithfulness as individuals proclaims God as better than our money and his command to give as more delightful than our desire to get.
2. As you invest your church's money in God's work, your congregation deliberates about which investments best align with the values God gives us in Scripture, often making investments the world says are foolhardy. Once again, you're showing off how good and trustworthy God is.
3. As God chooses to bless those investments, he shows himself to be a God of power, of mercy, and a God who keeps his promises.

Risky giving, value-based investing, and God's blessing are three main ways a budget can show off the glory of God. The first two of these engage our responsibility to be faithful. In the third, God brings glory to himself as he makes our work fruitful. Now I'll be honest, the more time I spend around churches, the more amazed (and appalled) I am at what kinds of things get done with "the glory of God" stamped on as justification. So think practically about what this means for your church. By looking at your church (who you are, what you do), people should be amazed at how good and excellent God is. That's what it means for God to get glory through your church.

Faithfulness and Fruitfulness

Having mentioned faithfulness and fruitfulness, it's important to understand how these two concepts relate to each other. Let's start by defining some terms.

Faithfulness is our responsibility to obey what God has asked us to do in the way he has asked us to do it. *Fruitfulness* is God producing results that please him. First Corinthians 3:6 is helpful in seeing this: "I planted the seed, Apollos watered it, but God has been making it grow." Sometimes Christians talk about faithfulness and fruitfulness as if they are in tension with one another: "We want to be fruitful, but not at the expense of being faithful." Yet the Bible never pits faithfulness against fruitfulness. Both are aimed at the same goal of showing off the glory of God.

Does this mean a faithful budget is simply a well-intentioned budget? No. Faithfulness is more than good intentions. Just because your intentions are good does not mean you have obeyed well. For example, you might discover that a missionary you've supported for years has been teaching a false gospel all that time. Will you be counted as faithful on the last day because you *thought* he was doing good gospel work? That probably depends on whether you could have had better, more obedient stewardship. What if you'd spent more time getting to know that missionary before you funded him or been more involved in his ministry? Your intention may have honored God, but because you were not careful in your obedience, what was done with your money dishonored him.

On the other hand, does this mean that if a church has been faithful with its budget, it should ignore fruitfulness because "that's God's job, not ours"? Again, the answer is no. Faithfulness *normally* bears fruit. Certainly it's possible to be faithful and not bear fruit. Beyond that, God sometimes has different fruit in mind than what we expect. Sometimes his timeline is longer than what we thought. Yet if, as God says, his Word "will not return to me empty, but will ... achieve the purpose for which I sent it" (Isa. 55:11), then we should expect that the ministry of God's Word will normally bear fruit. In this, our work is like gardening. If my plant is unhealthy, I can't be sure that it was my fault, but I should strongly suspect that I did something wrong. And if I do see healthy plants, I give praise to God because he's the one who gave the growth; all I did was follow the rules.

As you can see, faithfulness draws into its scope both the end and the means. We are faithful if we obediently aim at the right ends. We are faithful if we obediently pursue the right means. Your church budget matters both because of the work it seeks to fund and because of what funding that work says about Christ's work in you.

Faithful to Do What?

To summarize, God's goal for your church budget is that through your faithfulness he will get the glory. But, you might ask, what must we be faithful to do? As a church, what commands are we to obey? What promises should guide the risks we take?

The first part of this answer depends on how we define the word *church*. Sometimes the New Testament uses that word to describe all the individual Christians who are part of a local church, using *church* as a collective noun. In that sense, the church's task is as broad as God's calling on every person. We live out the Christian life as spouses, friends, and evangelists, in our varied roles as police officers, farmers, homemakers, or accountants, as caretakers of creation, society, and so forth. In this, we follow a general biblical call to love our neighbors as ourselves.

But that's not the sense of "church" we're using when we talk about a church budget. When we talk about church budgets, we use the term *church* in its more institutional sense. That is, the special way the Bible says Christians represent Christ when they gather together as the local church. What is the job of the church in this sense?

Fortunately, we need not stray far from Matthew 25 to find the answer. In Matthew's gospel Jesus gives us his clearest teaching on who the church is and why it exists. Jesus inaugurates the church in Matthew 16:18: "On this rock I will build my church, and the gates of Hades will not overcome it." He defines the church in chapter eighteen as a committed fellowship of those with a credible claim to follow Christ: "For where two or three gather in my name, there am I with them" (v. 20). And then in Matthew 28:18–20 he famously commissions his church: "All authority in heaven and on earth has been given to me. Therefore go and make disciples of all nations, baptizing them in the name of the Father and of the Son and of the Holy Spirit, and teaching them to obey everything I have commanded you. And surely I am with you always, to the very end of the age."[1]

To put it simply, the job of your church collectively is captured in the command of Matthew 28. You are to make, baptize, and equip disciples of Jesus.

What Difference Does Faithfulness Make?

Let's put all this together. First, God doesn't need your money. He doesn't need your church's money. And yet your church has the wonderful opportunity to glorify him as it spends its money. How? By investing in the command and promise of the Great Commission. That's faithfulness. And that's God's goal for your church budget. That's why God cares about your church budget, to answer the question in the title of this chapter. Yet orienting your church's budget around God's goal of faithfulness is not an easy task. We're so drawn to the idea that the budget matters because of what it can accomplish. So, practically, how do we ensure that being faithful to God shapes our thinking about the budget? Consider six truths to remember:

Remember that size is secondary. Earlier I mentioned that God is not impressed with the size of your church's budget. No matter how orthodox your theology, there's probably something in you that counts "nickels and noses" to validate your church's ministry. Yet these are no

---

1. Note the textual connections that hold these three passages together. In Matthew 16, Jesus says he will give his followers the "keys of the kingdom of heaven; whatever you bind on earth will be bound in heaven, and whatever you loose on earth will be loosed in heaven" (v. 19). What are these keys? That remains a mystery until chapter 18 when we learn that they represent authority to designate which of Jesus's followers have a *credible* profession of faith in him—authority of designation that Jesus gives to the local church. These two passages about the church, in other words, are all about Jesus entrusting his authority to the local church. The Great Commission also begins with a statement of Jesus's authority. So, not surprisingly, when those who heard that Commission began to live it out in the book of Acts, they did so by planting churches.

guarantee that you are being faithful. This doesn't mean size is imma-
terial. Sometimes an unimpressive budget indicates a lack of faith. But
for too many of us, the church budget (and building and attendance
and baptisms) is a personal Tower of Babel, a monument to ourselves
and our achievements instead of to God and his glory.

Remember that church health matters more than church size. If the
budget of your church fuels church growth at the cost of self-centered
consumerism, it can hardly be judged as faithful in God's sight. Quite
often, a church that struggles to reach critical mass is a sign that the
ministry is not healthy. But sometimes, small is beautiful.

Remember that God often works through your limitations. How
often have you complained about the limitations of your church's
budget? I certainly have. "If these people would just give an extra 20
percent, look at how much we could do!" "If the congregation would
just give an extra $100,000, we wouldn't lose our building." Why
would a sovereign God allow those limitations? Think of how often
in Scripture it is the limitations that reveal the glory of God. Consider
Gideon's tiny army, David's simple slingshot, and Jesus's clueless
disciples. Faithfulness is both aggressive in the risks it takes and content with the limits God ordains.

*Remember to motivate giving in the congregation based on opportu-
nity, not need.* A faithfulness mentality trusts that God will meet every
need that needs meeting, and we are just fortunate to have the opportunity to come along for the ride. Yet instead, many churches ground
their appeals for giving based on need. "We *must* do something about
[name your need]." With a faithfulness mindset, we give not because
needs must be met but because God must be glorified.

Remember that God cares about how *things are done.* If the budget process is dominated by a tyrannical pastor or is cobbled together
from the interests of competing church factions, it hardly shows off
the goodness and glory of God. A faithfulness mentality recognizes
the importance of *how* we manage the budget (how we assemble it,
how we give toward it, how we use the money).

Remember to listen carefully to God's Word. Instead of obsessing about using our money "effectively," faithfulness obsesses about aligning our practices with the Bible's principles—things like paying pastors and planting churches. A faithfulness mentality takes its cues heavily from Scripture rather than simply doing whatever seems best and trusts that in the long run, obedience is the most effective thing we can do.

A focus on faithfulness changes all aspects of your church's budget. Think of the joy this mentality gives us! If you approach the budget with an accomplishment mentality, when is there reason to rejoice? Only when the budget accomplishes its goals, right? But consider how much more joy a faithfulness mentality brings. We rejoice when God is glorified through our giving. We rejoice when God is glorified through a risk-taking, obedient budget. And then we rejoice when we see God bearing fruit from those investments because we have the privilege of being the means to his glorious end.

Conclusion: The One Thing That Matters

A focus on faithfulness is liberating because it means that no matter the complexity or size of your church's budget, there is just one thing that matters. Whenever I think about or talk about or work on my church's budget, I have one primary concern in mind. I am looking ahead to that final conversation that each member of my congregation will one day have with Jesus about how they've invested their lives. I'm thinking about their final accounting: will they be found faithful? It is no light matter that the members of my congregation—and yours—commit to our churches a significant portion of their wealth every year for investment in the Great Commission. May your people be thankful on that last day for every dollar they entrusted to your church's budget.

CHAPTER TWO

LEADERSHIP

Budgeting Is Pastoral Work

In November 2016 the government of India declared all five hundred- and one thousand-rupee banknotes to be null and void. Imagine the US government deciding the country will no longer use ten- and twenty-dollar bills and declaring that any you have are suddenly worthless. To add to the chaos, all of this happened with just four hours' notice![1] What do you do with your five hundred- and one thousand-rupee notes after hearing that announcement? You move quickly to trade! You trade what's of passing value as fast as you can for a currency that will last.

This is a marvelous picture of Christian stewardship.

Your Church Budget as a Spiritual Mutual Fund

The day after your last day on earth, every bit of money you've accumulated over your lifetime will be of no value to you. You can't take it with you. But as author Randy Alcorn is famous for saying, you *can* send it on ahead. Just like those Indian merchants busily exchanging

---

1. Vidhi Doshi, "India withdraws 500 and 1,000 rupee notes in effort to fight corruption," *The Guardian*, November 8, 2016, https://www.theguardian.com/world/2016/nov/08/india-withdraws-500-1000-rupee-notes-fight-corruption. The government gave its people fifty days to exchange their now-unusable notes for new ones with a limit of four thousand rupees (about US $60) per exchange. The purpose of the move was to combat currency forgery and to hamper the underground economy.

now-worthless currency, you can exchange worldly wealth for treasure in heaven, "where moths and vermin do not destroy, and where thieves do not break in and steal" (Matt. 6:20). How? By using the money you now have to show off the goodness of the Master. You might use your soon-to-be-worthless money to obey God's command to provide for your family (1 Tim. 5:8). Or use it to care for those in need (1 John 3:17). You might decide to give it to support the ministry of your church (Gal. 6:6). Or ideally, all of these things!

Think of your church budget as a long-term mutual fund with an excellent rate of return. It's a *spiritual* mutual fund. If you don't know how a mutual fund works in the financial world, it's simple. Thousands of investors entrust their savings to an investment manager. Then, that manager looks for the best investments that fall in line with the fund's investment goals. When it's time for an investor to cash out, they expect to see a return on that initial investment.

Do you see the similarities? The members of your congregation faithfully give a portion of the wealth and money they have each year to the ministries of your church. As a church, you look for the best way to invest that money for God's kingdom, making investments that are faithful to the Great Commission. Someday, each of these saints will stand before the Lord to give account for how they've stewarded what he entrusted to them (2 Cor. 5:10), and they anticipate a heavenly return on that earthly investment.

That places a big responsibility on those who manage that fund. Consider the great sum of money your church will invest in God's kingdom over its lifetime. How can you steward that money well? Stewardship begins with leadership. So who should lead the budget process, and how should they lead?

Spiritual Investing Requires Spiritual Leaders

To answer this question, we need to return to the goal we looked at in chapter one. God's goal for your church budget is *that your*

congregation be found faithful in their calling to the Great Commission.
And remember, this concept of faithfulness has two components:

- Obedience: faithfulness trusts that God's commands in
  Scripture are always the best course of action.
- Risk: faithfulness takes risks by funding investments the world
  belittles but that God says are valuable (say, funding church
  planting in a closed country).

A church budget can be administratively complex, covering many
different ministries and affecting large numbers of people. But it is
even more *spiritually* complex. The commodities we're dealing with
(eternal reward, faith, obedience) demand spiritual discernment.
If church budgeting were simply a matter of stewarding physical
resources, a committee of administratively-minded church members
would be the ideal leadership team.

But church budgeting is about faithfulness to God. Rather than
delineating between "physical" and "spiritual" areas of administration, the New Testament views spiritual and physical affairs of the
church as comprising one integrated ministry.[2] The physical concerns
of a church nearly always align with spiritual concerns, and these concerns require an eternal perspective. As a result, a church is a spiritual
institution with spiritual investment goals, and it should have Spirit-
minded leadership.

This has an important implication: *the church budgeting process
should be led by the church's pastors and elders.* Why? Because these
are the leaders who have been chosen because they possess spiritual discernment (having met the qualification of Titus 1:9), and
they have been tasked specifically with caring for the spiritual well-
being of the congregation (Heb. 13:17). The decision to entrust the
spiritually-fraught questions of budgeting to administratively-focused

---

2. Cited from an unpublished memo by Gustav Pritchard, pastor of Emmanuel Baptist
Church in Roodepoort, South Africa.

committees is at the root of much budget-related dysfunction. For the purposes of this book, I'm using terms like *pastor* and *elder* interchangeably.[3] That means I'm saying all pastors are elders and all elders are pastors, regardless of whether or not they are paid or hold a staff position at the church.

Now, you may be thinking, "But you don't know my pastor, Jamie. There's not an administrative bone in that body!" Or perhaps *you're* that administratively-deficient pastor. Fortunately, a pastor need not work alone. Let's look at a biblical example to see how spiritual and administrative leadership should work together.

Acts 6: Multiple Roles in Tackling Administrative Tasks

The story of the first deacons in Acts 6:1–7 illustrates what a healthy interaction of pastors, deacons, and the congregation might look like.[4] The problem at hand was, by all appearances, administrative: the church was allegedly overlooking the physical needs of some of its widows. But beneath that surface-level concern was a deeper, more spiritually-significant problem—the problem of disunity. The widows in question were in the Greek-speaking minority in a majority Hebrew church. So in response to this problem, the apostles told the congregation to select seven deacons to solve these problems. The congregation gladly obliged, and the situation was addressed.[5]

Using this passage as a guide, we must first consider the role of pastors/elders: pastors *lead*. In Acts 6, the apostles—who were temporarily

---

3. See how Paul speaks of the roles of shepherd (from which we get our word "pastor"), overseer (from which we get our word "bishop"), and elder as one and the same in Acts 20:17, 28.

4. Chapter seven, on operations, has a more thorough examination of this passage.

5. Because the role of deacon is treated as a church office elsewhere in the New Testament (e.g., 1 Tim. 3:8–13; Phil. 1:1), the roles described in this passage seem to be intended at least in some ways as normative. However, it would be stretching the intent of this passage to read into it prescription about church offices that extends beyond the highest-level description of their roles. As such, I am treating Acts 6 in this chapter as a wise example and not as detailed prescription for our churches today.

acting as elders in the Jerusalem church[6]—led by defining the problem. Beneath the surface-level problem of unequal treatment was the real problem as they saw it. It was the problem of disunity, and it carried with it the potential for distraction since the apostles knew they must not neglect the teaching of God's Word. They also led by asking for seven deacons who would provide administrative leadership to address this problem. Why seven? Presumably so the church would not simply give equal representation to Hebrews and Hellenists. The selection of seven leaders would force them to address the disunity problem.

The idea that pastors would lead in administrative matters is certainly not limited to this passage, of course. Elders are sometimes called overseers (Acts 20:28; Titus 1:7), a term that implies general administration of the entire local church.[7]

Similarly, in your church, I recommend that pastors give leadership to any administrative matters that have spiritual dimensions— including the budget. Pastors should identify the spiritual priorities at stake in the church budget and then lead the process of assembling a budget at whatever level of detail is necessary to address these spiritual priorities. In many churches, either for practical reasons or out of biblical conviction, there are multiple pastors, while in some churches one individual carries this responsibility alone. Either way, every church should do whatever it can to include a plurality of pastors/ elders in leadership, even if there is only one pastor on staff. What pastor wants to tackle the budget process alone?

Next, consider the role of deacons: deacons *support*. Even though pastors lead, they are generally wise to enlist the help of deacons who can assist them in administrative matters. As in Acts 6, deacons should support the leadership of the pastors, meaning there is no "balance of powers." Instead, we all work together under King Jesus, and Jesus has

---

6. By Acts 15:2, the Jerusalem church had elders who were not apostles.

7. The Louw-Nida Greek Lexicon explains that *overseer* captures both "the responsibility of caring for the needs of a congregation as well as directing the activities of the membership." Thus Paul instructs the young pastor/overseer Timothy on which widows qualify for church support in 1 Timothy 5.

clearly named a church's pastors as his undershepherds (1 Pet. 5:2). The deacons implement and assist in executing the priorities that the pastors/elders establish. For example, in Acts 6 we see the apostles establishing two priorities: to protect unity in the congregation and to protect their own teaching ministry. Whatever administrative solution the deacons develop is to serve those two priorities.

Finally, we should consider the role of the congregation: the congregation *actively follows*. In Acts 6, their role can be best summarized as following the apostles' leadership. Yet their following was not mindless; they selected the deacons. This is different from a church where the congregation's role devolves into simply doing what they're told. But it's also quite different from what we find in many churches, where "challenging, critiquing, and contending" would be better descriptions of congregational involvement than "following." And sadly, it's often the budget that proves to be one of the most contentious meetings of the year. If on the whole you can't trust your pastors with your money, why on earth are you trusting them with your soul? To be more specific, I believe the congregation's role should be threefold in regard to the church budget.

First, the congregation provides input. Wise pastors will ask the congregation for feedback and ideas as they assemble a budget. This can be an open call for suggestions, a congregational meeting focused on providing budget feedback, a time for more extensive feedback from a smaller group of members, or all of the above.

Second, the congregation gives. In a nonreligious civic organization, people give as they feel so inclined based on the worthiness of the cause. But the church is different. Giving to one's church is a basic discipline of the Christian life (Gal. 6:6). If someone feels they can't in good conscience give to their church, something almost certainly needs to change. They must either educate their conscience (so they *can* give) or find a new church. They don't need to love every item of the church budget, but they must obey the Bible's exhortations for them to trust their church leaders and to follow them (Heb. 13:17).

Third, a congregation should sometimes reject the budget. The congregation's role as followers is never absolute. When forced to choose, they must always obey God rather than people (Acts 5:29). So how does that apply to the church budget? Remember from chapter one that a church is accountable for faithfulness to the Great Commission. That is, its job is to protect and preserve the gospel so it can pass it on. When pastors propose something that is a clear and present danger to that calling—like the financial priorities and decisions reflected in a church budget—Scripture calls on the congregation to act.

For example, a budget might fund antigospel priorities—destroying a church's ability to protect the integrity of the gospel. Or a budget could be so financially precarious as to push the church into bankruptcy—destroying its ability to pass on the gospel. In some churches, this "emergency brake" role of the congregation is baked into polity and bylaws. Other congregations exercise it simply by voting with their feet (leaving). But regardless of polity, this authority is real in every church—and in few places is it more obvious than with the church budget.

The simple fact that the congregation will be doing the giving suggests that they should have an opportunity to accept or reject the budget—or at least provide feedback before it's finalized.[8] Of course, there are wise and unwise ways to involve the congregation. You want their feedback and their ownership; you don't want a budget being drafted by a committee of the whole. (For further reference, appendix A contains sample budget processes from churches of multiple denominational alignments, and appendix B contains sample language for a church's bylaws on congregational approval of a budget.)

---

8. To put these principles into practice, consider writing them into your bylaws. For example, include a statement that the budget must be proposed by the pastors, but, after a set period of time for feedback, it must be accepted by majority vote of the members. Also include a statement disallowing budget amendments from the floor during a congregational meeting so that the congregation's formal role is limited to an up or down vote on the entire budget.

Common Mistakes in Budget Leadership

Acts 6 shows a church working together to resolve an administrative matter with spiritual ramifications. Sadly, church budgeting practices often fall far short of such harmony. There are a few common errors to avoid.

The first can be called "Tyranny by the Pastor." You may have a picture in your mind of what this might look like. Essentially, the pastor determines the budget, and everyone else gets out of the way. Note, however, that this tyranny isn't always malevolent. Sometimes pastors fall into this error simply because the congregation trusts them. As the point person in my church for drafting the budget, I've found that people trust me—sometimes too much! Yet as Proverbs reminds us, "victory is won through many advisers" (Prov. 11:14). Here are some practices I've adopted that help me to steward that trust well and prevent any one person from controlling the budget process.

- When my church's pastors meet to assemble a proposed budget, I try to speak as little as possible—even though the rough draft they're reviewing is my work.
- I have conversations ahead of the budget meeting with many different church members so that my work represents more than just my own thoughts.
- When I disagree with a proposed budget idea, I must consider whether I can voice my concern without stifling further conversation, which often leads me to keep my mouth shut. Trust is wonderful, but it requires careful stewardship.

The second error to avoid is "Tyranny by Committee," where the group responsible for assembling the budget becomes all-controlling. This can leave the congregation feeling a lack of ownership in the budget, which is problematic since they're the ones who are supposed to give toward it. Beyond that, overdominance by a small group negates the God-given "emergency brake" role that the congregation has in reviewing the budget. A wise committee will invite feedback—both formally and informally—before finalizing the numbers and details. Remember, a church's leaders should function as pastors, not a board of directors.

A third error to avoid is what I call "A House Divided." In some churches, budgets are assembled to appease competing factions in the church. One line item satisfies the missions-minded, another is there for young families, and so forth. It's the church version of pork-barrel legislation in a dysfunctional democracy. Or you might find the pastors/elders and deacons/trustees acting as competing decision-making authorities—seeking to limit the other's power. But this reflects a worldly mentality. As Jesus notes, a house divided cannot stand (Mark 3:25). And remember Hebrews 13:17: the job of a congregation (including the deacons) is to help its leaders' work to be "a joy, not a burden, for that would be of no benefit to you." A congregation should free its pastors to lead!

Which of these three is your church most likely to fall into? What can you do about that?

What Does Pastoral Leadership Look Like?

Let's assume you agree that budget leadership should come from the pastors. That leads to another important question: What does good budget leadership look like? When does "oversight" become micro-management? When does "delegation" become abdication? The best level for a pastor to be involved at will vary from church to church. A small church where the pastor doesn't have much administrative assistance might require heavier involvement in the details of the budget. At a larger church where pastors are aided by competent, administratively-minded helpers, the pastors and elders might take a higher-level approach. Yet in every scenario, there are some roles pastors should play in leading the budget process.

BUDGET TASKS FOR PASTORS

1. Set the budget's income estimate.
2. Determine if high-level allocations are right.
3. Provide quality control for each budget line.
4. Balance long-term plans with emerging opportunities.
5. Assess unique opportunities for ministry.
6. Communicate the budget.
7. Break the budget.

The Budget's Income Estimate

When estimating a church's income, you will need to answer three basic questions to balance pastoral considerations with administrative realities.

1. What level of income should you expect from the congregation if they continue giving at current rates? You may well delegate this administrative question to others.
2. Is there a unique opportunity in this year's budget (such as a church plant) that would induce you to ask the congregation to give beyond their normal gifts? Or are there factors that would suggest lowering expectations?
3. Do you think the congregation is being faithful in their giving? You'll read more about the pastoral exercise of setting income expectations in the next chapter.

High-Level Budget Allocations

Does the portion of the budget devoted to any large categories of investment (e.g., facilities, outreach, staff) need to change? If so, how fast does it need to change? For example, perhaps you think that as your congregation matures spiritually, its desire to fund church planting will grow at the expense of facilities improvements. Or perhaps you think you are overinvested in missions and outreach such that you are neglecting your own congregation (which over time will limit your ability to do outreach and missions).

Basic Quality Control

How well is the church's money being invested? Remember, this is a spiritual mutual fund you're running. For example, perhaps the budget funds a weekly breakfast for marketplace professionals. Is it right for the entire congregation to subsidize what those individuals can pay for themselves? That's not an administrative question but a pastoral one.

Sometimes there are items in your church's budget that your pastors would like to defund, but the political capital you'd expend to get there is too high. That's okay. Keeping your church together is nearly always more valuable than having a "perfect" budget (Eph. 4:3). But do you have a plan for getting to a more spiritually valuable budget over time? Sometimes for the sake of one ill-tempered sheep, a pastor tempts the entire flock to grumble since it's clear to everyone else that a certain line item is a poor use of money.

Part of a pastor's quality control job is to determine which good things a church should not fund simply because it's a *church*. Remember: the church's job is the Great Commission. A good rule of thumb to keep in mind: Are there items in the budget that non-Christians are interested in funding? If there are, praise God for his common grace! In general, focus your efforts on causes only Christians will get behind.

Balancing Long-Term and Emerging Opportunities

Our church has long-term plans to renovate our building and train new pastors. Yet a few years ago, a beloved former pastor of ours moved back to the area to plant a church in a nearby neighborhood. We gladly adjusted our renovation and training plans to fund the new church.

Would you say your church grips too tightly to its long-term plans at the expense of new budget opportunities? Or do you lack sufficient multiyear planning? A good plan doesn't need to be overly detailed or involved. Even a bare-bones plan is helpful in anticipating staff changes, facilities needs, church plants, and more.

Evaluating Unique Opportunities

Every church will find some investment opportunities that it is especially well-positioned to pursue. There are several factors you might take into account in determining how well suited an investment opportunity is for your church:

- *Your location.* Would an opportunity benefit from your congregation's knowledge of one area of the world (such as your own neighborhood or another place you know well)?
- *Your relationships.* Sometimes your church can invest in an opportunity better than others because of the relationships you've built. For example, my church has a long history of involvement in our denomination's missionary sending organization, so we are well equipped to support budget investments related to their work.
- *Your expertise.* Located in Washington, DC, my church is full of people involved in government. Several years ago, we learned of a missionary in a closed country who was advising that country's government as his platform for missions work. That was a good fit with our unique skills; our people were able to help this country toward better governance and share the gospel through the relationships they built in the process.
- *Your insights.* Perhaps in all humility you determine that your church has better ideas about some common challenges than most other churches. You feel you're particularly skilled in disaster relief or in counseling or in doing children's ministry.
- *Your pastor.* Take the gifts and interests of your main preaching pastor into account when making budget decisions. If your

church is built around God's Word, the leadership of the individual who handles God's Word the most will matter more than other pastors or members, and your pastor will lead best in areas where they feel most excited and confident.

SKEPTICAL ADVICE ON ALIGNING
BUDGETS WITH STRATEGY

A useful concept from the world of business is that budgeting should be directed by strategy. That is, what you're trying to do should dictate how you invest your money. However, be careful how you apply this principle to a church because every church has essentially the same strategy. What do I mean by this? In business, a strategy boils down to two fundamental components: your target market and your source of competitive advantage. But those two items are the same for every church. Your "target market" is whomever God brings through your doors and your "competitive advantage" is the gospel. As a result, when a church tries to *create* a "strategy," it can inadvertently replace these two fundamentals with something else. For example, your target market becomes "young families" and your competitive advantage becomes "great children's ministry." But with that as your strategy, what's happened to the diversity that should be a hallmark of the church? And are you now attracting people by the strength of a program instead of the power of the gospel? More on this in chapter five. Every church will have its own unique personality, largely based on its unique opportunities for ministry as outlined in the previous section. But be careful that you don't end up with a unique strategy.

These first five roles all relate to the assembly of an annual budget. To help you put this into practice, I've gathered many of these principles into the Budget Discussion Worksheet you'll find at the end of this chapter.

Budget Communication

Beyond the first five roles involved in assembling a budget, there are two additional roles that pastors should play, starting with communication. A budget is full of opportunities to teach about spiritual priorities. Don't waste that opportunity! Since the Bible gives pastors the primary responsibility for teaching, they should generally take responsibility for communicating about the budget. I've devoted the last chapter of the book to this topic.

Deviations from the Budget

Sometimes emergency spending forces a church to break its budget. In that case, pastors should lead the decision of *how* to break the budget. Should the church reallocate money from other commitments, make a special appeal for funds, or dip into its reserve fund or line of credit?

On the other hand, at times the decision to break the budget is more opportunistic. For example, an opportunity emerges midyear to hire a highly qualified staff member. Is the spiritual value of that opportunity worth the cost? Remember, the pastor's job isn't to protect the budget at all costs but to be faithful with gospel opportunities, even those you didn't foresee when you drafted the budget.[9]

Conclusion: Praying through Your Budget

There is so much pastoral judgment that goes into budgeting! If you're a pastor, my hope is that you'll make it your ambition to know

---

9. My church has a general rule of thumb for breaking the budget that we've found useful: budget deviations of five thousand dollars or less can be made by our administrative pastor; deviations from five thousand dollars to a second, higher threshold are made by the elders as a whole; any changes beyond that must be approved by the congregation. Of course, those levels are suited to the specifics of my congregation.

the church budget as well as anyone else in the church. You might consider using it as a prayer guide. Perhaps one day each week, pray through a different line item or category of the budget and ask God to accomplish the gospel ambitions that stand behind that money. If you're not a pastor, use these thoughts to better support your pastors in their budgeting work.

A great example of how budgeting abounds with pastoral dilemmas is the first step of budgeting—to determine how much money your church has to work with. That's the topic we will focus on in the next chapter.

Budget Discussion Worksheet

Download an editable copy of this form at
https://www.9marks.org/budgetresources.

Complete the Income, Allocation, and Debt tables. Distribute copies of this worksheet to those responsible for drafting the budget. Compile results to assist with discussion at the beginning of the budget process.

INCOME	Year			
	20___	20___	20___	20___
Median or average giving per member	$	$	$	$
Per-member giving growth minus inflation	%	%	%	%
Portion of total giving from top 5% of givers	%	%	%	%
Portion of members not giving	%	%	%	%
Income as % of prior-year income	%	%	%	%

- What are some positive signs of faithfulness in our giving?

- What concerning trends do we see?

- What factors do we think may be driving those trends?

ALLOCATION OF EXPENSES	% of Current Budget	Ideal %
Staff		
Admin/Facility		
Programs/Ministry		
Outreach (int'l)		
Outreach (local)		

- Does this allocation seem sustainable over the next five years?

- If not, what will increase, and what should decrease as a result?

- Does this allocation seem wise over the next five years?

- If not, what should increase, and what should decrease as a result?

- How will we go about making these shifts in allocation?

LINE ITEM REVIEW

- Which line items in the current budget do you find *least* compelling?

Line Item	Amount	Category
1.	$	
2.	$	
3.	$	

- In your opinion, what are the most compelling items that didn't make it into this budget?

Line Item	Amount	Category
1.	$	
2.	$	
3.	$	

- Are there any items in the budget that are unwise or inappropriate, perhaps because we are a church (vs. another civic organization)?

- Which items being considered for the budget will be the most controversial and therefore threatening to the unity of the congregation?

DEBT

Interest on debt as portion of total spending:	%
Outstanding principle as % of total church assets:*	%

Assessing our current level of debt:	Disagree	Neutral	Agree
• It is constraining current ministry.			
• It will likely constrain future ministry.			
• It is impairing our congregation's view of debt.			

---

* Not including the value of the church building, if you own one. I would discourage churches from seeing their building as a saleable asset.

CHAPTER THREE

INCOME

Aiming for Faithfulness

During budget season, one of the most challenging decisions you'll make is the number staring at you from the very top of the budget sheet. How much income should you expect to receive this year? Most of your church's income will likely come from your congregation's giving, and that's a difficult number to estimate.[1] Do you just assume this year's giving will follow last year's growth rate? Do you "stretch your faith" and budget for more? Do you play it safe and budget for less?

Faithfulness Matters More than Income

First, let me put you at ease about one thing: getting your income estimate right is less important than you might think. As I've told my church dozens of times, I care very little whether they meet our budgeted income. If the congregation is faithful in their giving but we still miss the budget, I'm elated. We will figure out how to adjust accordingly.

But let's flip that around. If the congregation is faithless in their giving and we still make budget, we've failed—no matter how many

---

1. Other sources of income could include rental income, event fees, gifts from donors outside your congregation, or even endowment income. For a description of some of the downsides of having a church endowment, read https://www.thegospelcoalition.org/article/you-asked-should-a-church-invest/.

good things we did with that money. What matters most is faithfulness, not how much money we give. Of course, the faithfulness of your congregation is something only God can fully measure. Yet there is still value in grasping and teaching this principle: faithfulness matters more than income. This is the mentality you want your church to have as you consider the top line of your church's budget.

Consider how the apostle Paul spoke to the Corinthian church on the subject of giving. It appears that the Corinthian Christians had committed to help struggling Christians in Judea (1 Cor. 16:1–2; 2 Cor. 8:10–11; 9:2), so Paul spends chapters 8 and 9 of his second letter to the Corinthians encouraging them (even haranguing them) to deliver on their promise. Yet Paul is careful here. He clarifies that the amount of money contributed doesn't matter nearly as much as their eagerness to give: "For if the willingness is there, the gift is acceptable according to what one has, not according to what one does not have" (2 Cor. 8:12). From God's perspective—the eternal perspective—faithfulness is what counts. How much we give matters mainly as an indicator of our faithfulness.

This is a simple principle, but its implications for your church's budgeting process are counterintuitive. Let me explain. Because faithfulness is the top priority, the income line of the budget should have very *little* to do with how faithful your congregation has been in their past giving. You should teach about financial faithfulness and pray for financial faithfulness—but then budget for whatever the congregation will actually give, regardless of whether or not that level of giving is faithful. To understand why, we need to debunk three common myths about budgets and faith.

Myth #1: A Bigger Budget is Evidence of More Faith

Does this conversation sound familiar?

BUSINESS MANAGER: "Based on last year's giving, we should expect total income next year to be about $600,000."

DEACON JOE: "But we're supposed to be people of faith, right? Why should our budget simply assume what we 'expect'? Let's stretch our faith and shoot for a million! God's bigger than our expectations, isn't he?"

PASTOR TOM: "Joe's right. I'm sure some in our congregation aren't giving as much as they should. We need a bigger budget if we're going to become faithful givers."

There is much to affirm in Deacon Joe's desire to stretch people to give. Deacon Joe believes in a God who is bigger than our financial limitations. Deacon Joe believes in giving to the local church. Given all this, my guess is that Deacon Joe is a big contributor to his church budget. We'd do well if we all had more Deacon Joes in our churches!

Yet Deacon Joe misunderstands the nature of faith. According to Hebrews 11:1, "Faith is confidence in what we hope for and assurance about what we do not see." Is faith confidence in *anything* we hope for? No. Next to the word *faith*, the most common key word in that famous "faith hall of fame" of Hebrews 11 is the word *promise*. Faith is assurance that God will do what he has *promised*. And Deacon Joe needs a gentle reminder that while God has promised many things, he has never promised the church a million-dollar budget. If I were talking with Deacon Joe, I might say something like, "Joe, you expect $600,000 but want to budget for $1,000,000. I love that desire! But would you respect me if I did that with my personal budget? That feels less like faith and more like presumption." Be careful not to cash checks that God hasn't written.

The "positive thinking" movement of the early twentieth century told us that if we believe something strongly or intensely or sincerely enough, we can make it happen. This concept became known as the "prosperity gospel," an antigospel message that if we have enough faith, we will be blessed with health and wealth in this life.[2] But even in

---

2. For an accounting of how positive thinking became the so-called prosperity gospel, read David Jones and Russell Woodbridge's *Health, Wealth & Happiness: Has the Prosperity Gospel Overshadowed the Gospel of Christ?* (Grand Rapids: Kregel, 2011) or, for a more in-depth version of that story, *Blessed* by Kate Bowler (New York: Oxford University Press, 2013).

Bible-believing churches like Deacon Joe's, the prosperity gospel can slip in. For example, by assuming that faith always implies bigger and better.

Let's consider the true nature of faith according to the Bible. What happened to the faithful saints in Hebrews 11? "They were put to death by stoning; they were sawed in two; they were killed by the sword. . . . These were all commended for their faith, yet none of them received what had been promised" (Heb. 11:37, 39). Deacon Joe reminds me of the people of Israel in Numbers 14. God tells them to invade Canaan against incredible odds. They refuse and rebel, so he consigns them to forty years of wandering. Realizing they've made a mistake, they immediately reconsider: "Now we are ready to go up to the land the LORD promised. Surely we have sinned!" (v. 40). But there's a problem. They are no longer backed by God's promise. Their attack is no longer faith but presumption, and they are defeated.

For a variety of reasons, Joe and Tom's church *might* aim at a million-dollar budget. But they should not call that decision "faith." Otherwise, they are communicating to their people that God will deliver on a promise he never signed up for.

THE PROBLEMATIC TITHE

Another way church leaders ascribe promises to God that he never made is by teaching that Christians will be blessed if they give 10 percent of their income. Consider the promise of Malachi 3:10: "'Bring the whole tithe into the storehouse, that there may be food in my house. Test me in this,' says the LORD Almighty, 'and see if I will not throw open the floodgates of heaven and pour out so much blessing that there will not be room enough to store it.'" If someone understands this verse to promise financial blessing for those who tithe, they are misreading it. Why?

- The tithe was part of old covenant worship instituted at Sinai. When Jesus came, he was the fulfillment of everything that system pointed to. The requirement to tithe is no more a part of our worship today than are animal sacrifices or a regular pilgrimage to Jerusalem.
- The New Testament never commands Christians to tithe. Jesus affirms the Pharisees for tithing (Luke 11:42), but, of course, they were under the old covenant. In fact, the old covenant expected more than 10 percent: the law described multiple tithes, and Malachi 3 expects more than just a tithe.[1]
- Jesus promises tremendous blessing for obedience both in this life and the next. But in this life he has also promised difficulty (Mark 10:30).[2]

Focusing on 10 percent leads those who can't/shouldn't give 10 percent to feel wrongly guilty and those who do give more than 10 percent to feel wrongly self-satisfied. Jesus's call is to give 100 percent. Every dollar is subject to king Jesus, not just 10 percent. I tell my congregation that 10 percent is a great place to start. After all, Jacob gave 10 percent long before the Law of Moses. But our stewardship neither begins nor ends with giving 10 percent.

Incidentally, church history also sounds a cautionary note in this regard. In his historical survey *Tithing in the Early Church*, Lukas Vischer traces attitudes toward giving through the centuries. He shows how a focus on freewill giving gradually gave way to a reintroduction of the Old Testament law of tithing as the church's financial needs increased and, as we also know, its grasp of the biblical gospel decreased. His summary? "The problem is that the reintroduction of the commandment to tithe not only dulls the sharpness of the challenge which Christ makes but also falsifies it in its very essence. Christ's challenge was diminished as soon as nothing more than the tithe was required; and its evangelical character was obscured when the amount of that which Christ challenges us to do was fixed *a priori*."[3]

---

[1] Note that the people are robbing God if they fail to give both tithes *and offerings* (Mal. 3:8).

[2] For a study of how Christians should view the tithe, you might read David A. Croteau, ed., *Perspectives on Tithing: Four Views* (Nashville: Broadman & Holman, 2011).

[3] Lukas Vischer, *Tithing in the Early Church* (Minneapolis: Fortress, 1966), 30.

Myth #2: A Bigger Budget Can Address a Lack of Faith

Do you recall the pastor's response to Deacon Joe? "I'm sure some of our congregation aren't giving as much as they should. We need a bigger budget if we're going to become faithful givers." It may be that this congregation is not faithful in their giving. Yet the budget is a remarkably ineffective tool for improving faithfulness!

Consider what happens if this church opts for a million-dollar budget. It's now ten months into the budget year, and the church is half a million dollars behind. Pastor Tom rebukes the congregation: "Remember, that commitment of a million dollars was a promise we made to God. Don't fail him now!"

If Tom's goal is to increase giving, that approach might well work. If his approach is to increase faithfulness, it's unlikely to succeed. After all, who's most likely to respond to a manufactured budget crisis? The people of the congregation who've been giving faithfully or those who haven't? My guess is the ones who've already been faithful. Through a combination of godly love and ungodly guilt, they will give beyond what they should—and still feel crushed when the church doesn't make budget. But guilt rarely motivates faithfulness, and most of the faithless will continue being faithless.

Remember, faithfulness shows off the goodness of God by betting on his promises in obedience to his commands. So it's *cheerful* giving that glorifies him (2 Cor. 9:7); guilty giving denigrates him. In that sense, the income line in the budget is more of a thermometer than a thermostat. It's an indication of your people's spiritual health, not a tool to make them healthier.

Myth #3: Spontaneity Equals Spirituality

When Paul taught the Corinthians how to give, he emphasized a deliberate approach to giving. It's something we should aim for as well. "On the first day of every week, each one of you should set aside a sum of money in keeping with your income, saving it up, so that when I come no collections will have to be made" (1 Cor. 16:2). Note that the apostle encourages giving that is regular: "On the first day of every week." It should also be planned: Paul tells them to "*set aside* a sum of money." And it should be progressive: giving should be "in keeping with your income."

There's nothing inherently wrong with special offerings and appeals for money. But when a church tries to bring in a significant portion of income that way, they may be tacitly contradicting the apostle's advice. Special appeals encourage giving in the heat of the moment rather than through a deliberation of how to use all our money for God's purposes. They encourage giving that is haphazard rather than regular. And they encourage a congregation to give without any consideration of what amount would be proportional to the money God has entrusted to them.[3]

---

3. To be responsible, you might make a special appeal for giving that asks your congregation to give only what is above and beyond their normal giving. But in my experience, people don't generally operate with that level of nuance. That kind of appeal might be wise for specific individuals you know well—but generally misleading for the congregation at large.

WHAT ABOUT ONLINE GIVING?

Are some methods of giving better than others? Does Scripture see a difference between putting cash in the offering plate and giving with your mobile phone? Consider the exhortation of 1 Corinthians 16:2, that giving be planned and deliberate. You may want to encourage giving methods that emphasize planning—like setting up an automatic, electronic withdrawal from a bank account. On the other hand, you should be wary of giving methods that promote haphazard, spontaneous giving—like a "give by text" system.

How Much Income Should You Assume in Your Budget?

With those three myths in mind, how *should* you budget for income? To put it simply: avoid the gimmicks, avoid manipulation, avoid false promises, avoid guilt. Teach and pray about financial faithfulness, then budget for whatever you expect the congregation to give based on their current maturity. Let's examine each of these: teaching, praying, and budgeting for what you expect.

Teach about Financial Faithfulness

If taught well, healthy and growing Christians will generally give faithfully. So teach about the wonderful opportunity we have to give! Your goal is for your congregation to see that following Jesus involves a right use of money. What topics should this teaching cover?[4]

---

4. Feel free to start with the class my church has written on this topic at https://www.capitolhillbaptist.org/classes (titled "Stewardship"). You can download the files for free and edit them as you wish. A good, quick-to-read book on this topic is Randy Alcorn's *The Treasure Principle* (Colorado Springs: Multnomah, 2008).

The Why

We don't give because we expect a financial return in this life, nor because we're obligated to donate a fixed portion of income. Instead, we give because we want to invest in what will last (Matt. 6:20), because giving brings spiritual blessing (Acts 20:35), because giving encourages others to be thankful (2 Cor. 9:12), because giving is the natural response of a grateful heart (2 Cor. 9:7), and because giving highlights the wealth God has given us in Christ (Matt. 13:46).

The How

Giving should be regular, planned, and progressive, as I mentioned earlier. In addition, giving should focus on the local church. "The one who receives instruction in the word should share all good things with their instructor" (Gal. 6:6). Since one's main source of teaching should be their church, the church should be the main recipient of one's giving. It's especially important in an age of individualism to submit giving to the wisdom of the church by giving primarily to its budget.

How Much

How much should we give? The short answer: *everything*. Wealth is not divided up between "mine" (90 percent) and "God's" (10 percent). Everything we have is from him (1 Tim. 6:17; 1 Cor. 4:7), and it is all to be used for his purposes (1 Pet. 4:10; 1 Cor. 10:31). I encourage my congregation to see 10 percent of income as a normal starting point for giving to our church. Some should give more than that since they've received proportionately more. But normally, all who have income should be giving substantively to their local church.

Has your teaching covered these three topics at some point in the last year? I don't suggest that you have a special sermon series on giving every year. With the frequency that both the Old and New Testaments address financial matters, faithful preaching through Scripture is ripe with opportunity to address money and giving, so if you're a preacher, try working the topic into your regular preaching and teaching. And in addition to public teaching, these topics may be good for one-on-one teaching as well. Can a church teach too much on giving? Absolutely. If your congregation is beginning to believe that you love them primarily for their money, you need to change your approach. I'll say a bit more on this at the end of this chapter.

In addition to teaching about money in your regular preaching ministry, make the discussion of giving and financial discipleship part of a robust membership process at your church. Membership formalizes the commitments the Bible calls every Christian to make to a church—including the commitment to give. Do you address stewardship in your new members class? Do you talk about it during pastoral interviews with prospective members? You need to talk about this with new members, both to encourage giving and to debunk the false preconceptions that many have about churches and giving (for example, that their responsibility stops at 10 percent, that God will bless them financially to the extent they give financially, etc.).

It can feel taboo to talk about money with our congregations, but we must! Jesus taught extensively about money, not because he wanted a handout but because he wanted our hearts. Disciple your people to find their ultimate treasure in Christ.

Pray for Financial Faithfulness

Earlier in this chapter, I mentioned three aspects of setting the income line of the budget: teach about financial faithfulness, pray for financial faithfulness, and then budget what you expect your congregation to give. Let's move on to the second of these. Quite simply, make it a regular point to pray for your congregation to give faithfully. You might do this in private, perhaps as part of praying through your church's budget over the course of a month. Or you might do this publicly, regularly leading the congregation in prayer for faithfulness in giving.

GIVING METRICS TO TRACK

If your goal is faithfulness (which only God can measure) does that mean you shouldn't track your church's giving? On the contrary, you'll shepherd better if you understand your congregation's giving. Here are four metrics you might consider tracking over time if you're able to do so.

1. *Per capita* giving by year. That is, giving per member.* Is *per capita* giving decreasing over time or increasing more slowly than inflation? That might be cause for concern. Are there clear explanations for that trend? For example, from a pastoral perspective, an influx of students or an economic recession would make you less concerned about a decline.
2. Percentage of the budget from your top 5 percent of givers. Is your church's budget increasingly reliant on just a few major givers? That should cause you to be concerned about the faithfulness of your congregation even if income and *per capita* giving look okay.
3. Percentage of family units who don't give.
4. How giving changes with membership tenure. Ideally, the longer someone is at your church, the more they will increase in spiritual maturity. Often, that maturity will be reflected in giving. Each year, I compare average giving by new members at my church with average giving by those who have been members for three to four years.

Discouraging trends in these metrics may have nothing to do with the faithfulness of the congregation. They may

---

* For the statistics-minded, *median* giving per capita is probably more useful to look at than *average* giving per capita.

simply evidence a shift in incomes or financial obligations. If you see negative trends, pray that your congregation will become more faithful if they aren't. You might increase the amount of time you give to teaching on financial faithfulness. If a negative trend is evidence of faithlessness in giving, then, sadly, faithlessness will likely show up elsewhere in the lives of your congregants as well. Positively, this means there will be many angles from which to address the issue of faithfulness.

Public prayer about giving is especially important because through it you can model how your members should think and pray about their own money and their own giving.[5] Here are a few ideas of what to pray for:

- That we would be overwhelmed by how much Christ has given to us.
- That we would give cheerfully, not out of guilt or obligation.
- That we would be wise in how much we decide to give.
- That we would give regularly, deliberately, and proportionately.
- That we would gladly part with what our world values in order to take hold of what God values.
- That our church would be wise in how it stewards our gifts.
- That our congregation would be known for its generosity.
- That our giving would show God to be good, delightful, and generous.
- That God would bring to fruition the hopes we have for every line in the church budget.

---

5. For more thoughts on this, you might read *Prayer: How Praying Together Shapes the Church* by John Onwuchekwa (Wheaton: Crossway, 2018), especially chapters six and eight.

Budget for the Giving You Expect

Having taught and prayed, use whatever financial model you find effective to determine how much you expect your people will likely give, and then set that as the top line of the budget.[6] You may find that having a financial advisory team of businesspeople in your church is helpful in forecasting this number.

Is that figure lower than you'd like, or even lower on a per member basis than other churches in your area? Don't despair! Remember, this is what God has given you. Some might suggest that the problem is an uninspiring budget. "People give to exciting causes." But we must recognize that faithfulness and "exciting" aren't *necessarily* related. Exciting budget items may extract more money from your people, but that doesn't mean they're giving out of love for God. And the best investments in your spiritual mutual fund may not look exciting at first glance. Instead, they may be more akin to the title of Eugene Peterson's classic book *A Long Obedience in the Same Direction*, faithfully continuing, year after year, out of obedience and conviction.

Your church members will become more faithful as God's Spirit works through prayer and his Word to grow them in maturity. Remember Romans 10:17, "Faith comes from hearing the message, and the message is heard through the word about Christ." If your congregation has a faith problem, the solution is not in your church's budget. It is in the patient work of God's Spirit through God's Word to convert and conform them to the image of Jesus Christ.

---

6. Most churches do not have a sufficiently large number of givers (i.e., sufficiently large data set) to warrant a very sophisticated model for predicting giving. Most likely, you're best off using a very simple model. For example, assume that *per capita* giving grows with inflation and that the size of your membership grows at the same rate as it did last year. Then adjust that figure for the factors listed in the "Factors to Consider" inset box below. You could get more sophisticated and segment out different bands of givers in your congregation, try to fit growth to a curve instead of a straight line, etc. But most likely, unless you have more than one to two thousand givers, that increase in sophistication will not likely give you a more accurate prediction of next year's giving.

FACTORS TO CONSIDER WHEN FORECASTING GIVING

Here are some questions to answer when estimating giving for the next year.

- Are there reasons to believe that the growth rate in the number of givers will be different next year than it was last year (e.g., you planted a church last year, filled your meeting space, your main preacher departed, etc.)?
- Are there reasons to believe that giving per giver will increase more quickly or slowly than inflation?
- Are you making changes in your church that will slow or reverse growth? Very often, as a church does the hard work to become healthier (clarifying the gospel, clarifying membership, etc.) it will experience some years of slow or negative growth. In that case, do you expect that those leaving are giving more or less on average than those who are staying and those who are coming?
- Is your giving highly dependent on a small number of givers? In general, if more than 50 percent of giving comes from your top 10 percent of givers, you'll want to be more conservative in estimating future giving.

Love Your People More than You Love Your Budget

Let me leave you with one final thought before the chapter closes. Make it clear that you love your people more than you love your budget. It's common sense, I know, but it's amazing how often the realities of church life push us in the opposite direction. Try this statement on for size: "I don't care nearly as much about meeting this budget as I do about the conversation you'll have with Jesus someday about faithfulness. I love all the good represented in our budget, but your faithfulness is much more important." Would that sound genuine coming from your mouth? Or do the staff and ministries in your church's budget loom so large in importance that keeping them afloat has become all-consuming? Remember: God doesn't need your money!

How can a church keep its priorities straight? Saying the words "I care much more about your faithfulness than about meeting this budget" can ring hollow if the congregation knows your back is up against the wall and you desperately need your church to meet the budget. So avoid having your back up against the wall! How can you do that?

In a word, try to keep your budget *flexible*.[7] Maintain a reserve fund (or at least a line of credit from a bank) that can allow you to absorb a budget shortfall over time rather than having to accommodate it immediately.[8] Many churches size their reserve fund as a certain number of months of operating expenses. This may make sense for an individual who can lose his job and will need to live off his savings while he looks for a new one. But the "months of operating expenses" rule is an odd fit for a church because a church is unlikely to lose all of its income suddenly. Instead, I recommend a church calculate its reserve fund in two pieces. First, determine the money you need to

---

7. Keeping the budget flexible is often a greater challenge for a church than it is for most businesses. Unlike a business, where costs are a mix of fixed (the same no matter your income) and variable (rising with more income and falling with less), most churches see nearly all their costs as fixed. That is, you anticipate that next year, like this year, you will be funding the same building, the same staff, the same ministries, the same missionaries. Changes in income that force changes in those fixed costs can be very painful for your congregation.

8. The Bible doesn't teach that it is necessarily wrong for a church to carry debt. However, many people in your church likely struggle with an ungodly attitude toward debt (e.g., debt as a savior instead of debt as a tool that we sometimes reluctantly use). So consider carefully how some in your congregation will understand your example when you use debt to manage cash flow, no matter the financial sense in what you're doing. A church has very different considerations to wrestle with than a business does when choosing to use a line of credit. But, of course, reserve funds take time to build, so a line of credit may appear to be the only option for your church. See inset in chapter seven for more thoughts on churches and debt.

balance cash flow through the year if you meet your budgeted income and expenses.[9] And second, determine the percentage of your church budget that is likely to fall short if income and/or expenses turn out to be different than what was budgeted.[10]

Another tool for maintaining budget flexibility is to budget for some one-time expenses that you hold until late in the year when you have a good sense for how income is progressing. These could be one-time grants to church planting projects, improvements to your facility, one-time gifts to organizations you support, or optional payments on a mortgage.

Be honest with the congregation when and where the budget *doesn't* have flexibility—and don't make this a regular occurrence. Sometimes you'll decide that a particular opportunity warrants having an aggressive income figure that you "need" to hit. For example, the decision to hire a new staff member or take on a building project will likely remove some flexibility from your church's budget for a time—even if expected income still covers your expected expenses. That's okay; just let the congregation know what's going on and recognize that this will make it harder to keep your priorities straight. Inflexibility should happen rarely and only after careful thought and prayer.

---

9. The first component of a reserve fund: the maximum negative cash flow your budget anticipates across the year. That is, let's say you bring in 30 percent of your income in December, but you spend money evenly across the year. That means that even if income and expenses exactly meet budget, your expenses will be greater than income at least through the end of November. The difference between year-to-date income and expenses on the day when your bank account is anticipated to be at its lowest point (say, November 30) is the first component of your reserve fund.

10. The second component of a reserve fund: the size of a likely budget net income "miss." For example, based on historical growth in membership and per-member giving, you determine that your congregation will most likely give at least 90 percent of your income target for the year and that, should you see a shortfall in income approaching, you could trim your expenses by 2 percent. In that case, the second component of your reserves should be 10% − 2% = 8% of your budget. Try to size your reserve fund based on "likely" possibilities. Unlikely possibilities (like a church split or a building fire or a financial implosion) will need to be dealt with as they arise. In that case, your congregation (and ultimately the providence of God) is your ultimate "reserve fund." For more detail on building a cash reserve fund, visit http://www.ecfa.org/Documents/Church_Cash_Reserves_(TCN%20Insight)_CHURCH.pdf.

INSULATE YOUR PASTORS FROM
KNOWING WHO GIVES WHAT

Church leaders often debate as to whether pastors should know who in the church gives how much. I think it can be good for the pastors to know who *doesn't* give—both to know who might need financial assistance and who might be in need of instruction about giving. However, I would argue that it's best for pastors not to know the size of their con-gregants' gifts. Why?

- For the sake of the pastor. Christians (pastors included) are not to show partiality to the wealthy (James 2:1–7). A pastor can certainly be impartial even if he knows that 10 percent of the church budget comes from one particular family. But not knowing that information in the first place lessens a common temptation.*
- For the sake of the giver. In my mind, this is even more important than reason number one. When a congre-gant knows that a large gift will catch the attention of a church leader they respect, that introduces some very dangerous motivations for giving. As Jesus said, let your giving be in secret (Matt. 6:3).

One way you can help your congregation believe that you love them more than their gifts is to insulate the pastors from the knowledge of how much each member gives.

---

* Of course, even if a pastor doesn't know the identity of this generous giver, it is important for him to know that a large portion of the church budget is dependent on one giver.

As delightful as it is to plan for a record year of giving, it's much better to *achieve* a record year of giving. Keep your income expectations in line with what is realistic and pray for God-exalting generosity in your congregation.

Conclusion: God Is Able

Paul's words in 2 Corinthians are an appropriate way for us to conclude this chapter. Are you discontent with what your church's budget is able to accomplish? Are you discontent with a worldly congregation that seems disinterested in giving? Hear God's encouragement to you: "God is able to bless you abundantly, so that in all things at all times, having all that you need, you will abound in every good work" (2 Cor. 9:8). The limits God has put around your church's budget are perfect. The pace at which he is growing your congregation's maturity is perfect. His plans for your church's future are perfect. He will perfectly accomplish his plans for your congregation, and in that promise is a wonderfully contented hope.

Of course, income is only one piece of the budget. The next few chapters walk through your major expense categories, beginning with staff.

STAFF

Supporting Servants of the Word

As a spiritual investment vehicle, your church budget has exciting prospects. Imagine the possibilities as you invest that money wisely year after year. It might be $200,000 a year, $2 million a year, or even $20 million a year. Regardless of the amount, handling the gifts given by God's people is a great privilege, isn't it?

If your church is like many other churches, a significant portion of that investment will directly fund church staff. And that makes perfect sense. After all, a church's goal is to be faithful to the Great Commission, and church staff are a significant part of "teaching them to obey everything I have commanded you" (Matt. 28:20). But when should your church hire staff? How many people should you hire? How much should you pay them? You must grapple with some very significant questions in this section of the budget.

A word of warning: in this chapter I work my way into some challenging questions (e.g., "at what point are we being overly generous in compensation?") by building up from first principles. So I would ask you to be patient as we work from what is clear and simple in Scripture to what is less clear and more complicated in its application to particular contexts.

Why Pay Any Staff at All?

Imagine if every church instantly liberated their budgets from the burden of paying their staff. If a typical church is spending half its money on staff, that would suddenly double the money available for everything else. You'd have twice as much money for international missions, for church planting, for mercy ministry—just like that!

Sounds compelling, doesn't it? But there's one slight problem with this utopian vision: the Bible. The New Testament never *commands* a church to hire a pastor, but it does *commend* it. Far from seeing a paid pastor as a necessary evil or optional accessory, the weight of the New Testament leans heavily toward paying for a pastor if at all possible. If you *do* pay your pastor, please don't skip this section! Understanding why you pay them is an important foundation for the other questions I'll address later in this chapter.

Consider Paul's teaching in 1 Timothy 5:17–18: "The elders who direct the affairs of the church well are worthy of double honor, especially those whose work is preaching and teaching. For Scripture says, 'Do not muzzle an ox while it is treading out the grain,' and 'The worker deserves his wages.'"

There are four observations we can make from these verses. First, when Paul speaks of the elders who "direct the affairs of the church well," he is speaking of a subgroup within the elders. That is, of all the elders, it is those who direct "well" who are worthy of double honor.[1] Second, notice that Paul explains that by "well" he means those "whose work is preaching and teaching."[2] The word

---

1. Like Baptists, most Presbyterians, and many other Protestants, I do not see two different offices in this passage—but I do see two different categories of elder. You might call them staff elders and nonstaff elders.

2. The word μάλιστα, translated "especially" in this translation, can also be translated "that is." Whether you read this as "especially" or "that is," Paul is using "labor in preaching and teaching" to better articulate what he means by "rule well." By translating μάλιστα as "especially," the work of "preaching and teaching" is a particularly good example of ruling well. By translating μάλιστα as "that is," the work of "preaching and teaching" is precisely what Paul means by ruling well.

translated *work* has the connotation of toil: labor that is intense and wearisome. Third, in verse 18, Paul cites Moses in Deuteronomy 25:4 ("do not muzzle an ox") and Jesus in Luke 10:7 ("the worker deserves his wages") to show that "double honor" includes compensation.

WHY PAY YOUR PASTOR?

1. To submit your church to Scripture (1 Tim. 5:17–18; Gal. 6:6).

2. To receive excellent Bible teaching. Over the last few years, I've spoken with hundreds of house church leaders in China about this issue. One of them described the foolishness of underspending on biblical teaching this way: "We want the very best. Only the best school. Only the best food. But it seems that for some of us, when it comes to Bible teachers, anyone will do."

3. To obey the Great Commission. The Great Commission isn't simply about making disciples somewhere *else*. It's also about teaching the disciples in *our* churches "to obey everything" Jesus has commanded us (Matt. 28:20). We should never get so excited about the first half of Jesus's command that we neglect the second half.

4. To have more money to invest. A full-time pastor can set aside more time to prepare excellent teaching. Excellent teaching equips the congregants to grow in godliness. As they grow, they will want to invest ever more deeply in gospel work. Paying your pastor may require cutting other spending today—but most likely in the long term it will free up more money for kingdom purposes, even if the congregation never increases in size.

And finally, note that Paul's justification for paying the elders who rule well lies not in their office (in which case all elders deserve compensation) or their financial need but in their labor ("The worker *deserves* his wages").

So what does this mean for your church? It means that in general, you should pay those who labor to provide teaching for your congregation. Of course, Paul himself sometimes went without the money he deserved (1 Cor. 9:12). But when he did so, his rationale was not one of financial frugality; it was because he didn't want young congregations to be confused by his pay (1 Cor. 9:12; 1 Thess. 2:5–10). Even then, he pointed out that his *not* being paid was the exception, not the norm (1 Cor. 9:6–7). In fact, he even goes so far as to describe his support by one church in the planting of another as "robbing other churches" (2 Cor. 11:7–8). Necessary sometimes, but not ideal: *normally, a church should support its own pastor.*

Some believe that if pastors are truly holy, they will do their work for nothing. But the biblical pattern begs to differ. It is to your benefit as well as theirs when you take responsibility for the cost of good teaching. "The one who receives instruction in the word should share all good things with their instructor" (Gal. 6:6). A Word-centered church is nearly always best off when it invests its money in excellent teaching of the Word. If it does, then see if, having invested in what is most important, "all these things will be given to you as well" (Matt. 6:33; cf. Luke 12:31).

When Should You Hire Additional Staff?

Beyond simply hiring a preacher, many churches have the money to hire multiple staff. But how should you evaluate these opportunities? I recommend that you begin with a clear understanding of the dangers of having additional staff. I realize that might surprise some of you. But here are a few examples to show you what I mean.

Let's say you hire a counseling pastor. The congregation breathes a sigh of relief when he arrives—now there's someone to take care of all the pastoral difficulties in the church! But as the counseling pastor assumes the care of needy people, he might deprive the congregation of ministry opportunities God has given them to build up the body of Christ into unity and maturity (Eph. 4:12–13). Instead of equipping the congregation to do the work of counseling and ministering to one another, a staff hire might replace that ministry and compromise the congregation's spiritual growth.

Or consider the hiring of a youth pastor. His much-needed enthusiasm quickly forms the teens into a tight-knit youth group with its own culture, its own worship band, and eventually, its own Sunday service. Everyone is thrilled that the teens love church again—but no one sees them anymore. Instead of a multigenerational body, you end up with, in effect, two distinct churches. A staff hire has compromised unity.

Does this mean you should never hire counselors or youth pastors? Of course not! My church has both, and they are wonderful blessings to our church. My point is that anytime you add a staff position, you must be aware of three potential dangers.

1. *Professionalization*: Staff can infantilize the congregation by *doing* ministry instead of equipping the *congregation* to do ministry. In fact, the very existence of a staff position can communicate to the congregation that "real" ministry belongs in the hands of trained professionals. Beyond this, don't underestimate the pressure on staff (whether conscious or not) to justify the value of their positions in ways that can obscure the real need for their work.

2. *Consumerism*: Staff can customize ministry for the preferences and needs of specific segments of the congregation. That may encourage a congregation's consumeristic tendencies, teaching them to value your church based on how well it meets their felt needs.

3. *Disunity*: Along similar lines, as staff pursue excellence in serving particular subgroups of the church, the congregation can begin to feel more like a loose collection of affinities and ministries instead of the body of Christ (1 Cor. 1:10–13).

Of course, staff can also work against these tendencies if you design their roles with care.

So when should you take ministry out of the hands of a volunteer and create a staff position instead? Here are several dos and don'ts when you are considering adding a staff position in your church.

First, *do* hire staff to free up the pastor(s). This is a biblical motive that we see in the establishment of the first deacons, who were selected to address a unity issue that was distracting the apostles from the ministry of God's Word (Acts 6:2). While this example refers to the establishment of deacons, it more broadly provides wisdom for hiring staff. A church might hire staff to support a pastor in focusing time on public teaching, individual shepherding, and prayer.

Don't hire staff to rescue the congregation from guilt over ministry it's not doing. Let's say your church is struggling with evangelism. It's tempting to hire a pastor for evangelism to "fix" this problem. But if the expectation is that the pastor will do the work of evangelism instead of the congregation, this hire will simply aid and abet their abdication of a God-given responsibility. In addition, you risk focusing the church quite narrowly on the initiatives this new pastor begins. It's best to teach on the priority of evangelism and pray for spiritual growth, then wait patiently for the Spirit to change hearts in your congregation. Once a concern for evangelism increasingly characterizes your congregation, you might hire a staff member to help facilitate the results and provide opportunities to equip and train people in the work of evangelism ministry.

When you're considering staff positions, *do* hire staff to serve the entire congregation. While each situation is unique, as a general rule it's best to avoid creating a staff position—and especially a pastoral staff position—dedicated to a narrow demographic within your congregation. Hire youth ministry staff who will focus on connecting youth and their families with other adults in the congregation. Hire a singles minister who will focus his time on integrating families into the lives of singles. You may need to make exceptions to this rule but do so carefully. Don't unwittingly institutionalize disunity.

Despite what some church experts recommend, *don't* staff up ahead of growth. Some have suggested that you can grow your church by staffing for the church you hope to have. But this approach intentionally keeps more staff on hand than are needed, which encourages the unhelpful downsides of staff positions, namely, doing the work of ministry instead of equipping others, and serving individual constituencies rather than the entire congregation. Staffing ahead of growth is often unavoidable when a church is starting out but can have serious downsides beyond that.[3]

Ask a few questions about each of the staff positions in the budget—or at least about new staff positions you're considering:

- Is this position designed to *do* ministry or to *equip* the congregation for ministry (Eph. 4:12)?
- Is this position designed to protect one or more of your pastors' time for ministry (Acts 6:2)?
- If this position were eliminated, would the congregation likely step in to do the work instead? Generally, if an activity is not important enough to get done if the staff position were eliminated, it is not important enough to get done.
- How much worse off would we be if we gave this job to a deacon instead of a paid staff member? I'm struck by how underutilized deacons are in many churches. Consider deacon roles that are defined in scope and limited in duration (e.g., a three-year term for deacon of student ministry). Within that design, your deacons can give themselves entirely to a particular ministry because they know it is only for a limited time—and they know they're responsible for it. That level of focus, in addition to the basic spiritual qualifications deacons must meet (1 Tim. 3:8–13) may entirely eliminate the need for a staff hire.[4]

---

3. For more guidance on the design of staff positions, read chapter eighteen in *The Deliberate Church* by Mark Dever and Paul Alexander (Wheaton: Crossway, 2005).

4. For guidance on structuring deacon responsibilities, read "The Committee-Free, Task-Specific Deacon" by Matt Schmucker at www.9marks.org/article/committee-free-task-specific-deacon/.

What I've written in this section pertains to both pastoral and administrative staff. Later in this chapter we'll look at some additional considerations for administrative staff.

How Much Should We Pay Our Staff?

One factor to consider when deciding how many staff your church should hire is the simple math of how much you pay them. Should you aim at lower compensation so you can hire more staff? What are the spiritual consequences of overpaying or underpaying your staff? Let me suggest two principles to guide your philosophy of staff compensation.

Generosity

Every time the New Testament addresses financial support of church staff and missionaries, it underscores generosity.

- "The one who receives instruction in the word should share *all good things* with their instructor" (Gal. 6:6, emphasis mine).
- "The elders who direct the affairs of the church well are *worthy of double honor*, especially those whose work is preaching and teaching" (1 Tim. 5:17, emphasis mine).
- "Do your best to speed Zenas the lawyer and Apollos on their way; *see that they lack nothing*" (Titus 3:13 ESV, emphasis mine).
- "Please send them on their way in a *manner that honors God*" (3 John 6, emphasis mine).

Don't be stingy with your staff compensation. What benefit is it to you for your pastor to be distracted from ministry because of financial needs?

It is possible to be overly generous as well. Extravagant pay is poor stewardship and may warp a pastor's motivations for ministry. After all, he is to be one who is "not pursuing dishonest gain, but eager to serve" (1 Pet. 5:2). So what constitutes pay that is generous but not extravagant? As with beauty, it would seem that "generous" is in the eye of the beholder. As such, Paul's exhortation in Titus 3:13 is a good summary of appropriate pay: "See that they lack nothing" (ESV). You shouldn't try to provide your staff with everything they could ever wish for. But you want to provide enough that a pastor or staff member is not distracted from ministry because of financial concerns.

HOW MUCH TO PAY ADMINISTRATIVE STAFF

I find it interesting that Paul's rationale to pay pastors in 1 Tim. 5:18 is not grounded in their office but in their work: "The laborer deserves his wages." As such, this principle offers rationale for paying administrative staff as well as a pastor. It implies that you should pay them what their work is worth, not how much you think they need. But shouldn't people working for a church make less money? No. If the laborer deserves his wages, he deserves what his work is worth. Evaluating what his work is "worth" might be complicated for a pastoral position, but it is comparatively straightforward for an administrative position. Since administrative jobs are often similar to positions in other nonprofit organizations and businesses in your area, you might find that regional compensation surveys conducted by the government are a good guide. Some struggling churches might not be able to pay market rate for a time. But over the long term, adjust your staff size to fit the available budget rather than asking a bloated staff to all work for less than their work is worth.

How can you be sure your staff are lacking nothing in this regard? I recommend five different data points that can guide your compensation decisions.

First, consider *nonchurch benchmarks*. How are comparable public servants paid? Similar to pastors, many public officials have agreed to work for less money than they could make on the open market. Yet like a church, their employers don't want them eventually forced into the private sector for want of money. You might find a useful comparison by looking at the compensation package of a local school principal or police chief, or the government pay scale.

You may also want to look at *church benchmarks*. How do other churches pay their staff? Several organizations will sell you benchmarking information for church staff positions in your area. Of course, churches are generally not known for being generous with their compensation. Don't assume that all or even most churches in your benchmarking set are being faithful in paying their staff. Rather than buying benchmarking data, you might find it more useful to exchange compensation information with a few churches in your area that you trust in this regard.

Consider what *replacement cost* would be for this position. If a staff member were to leave, would you need to increase (or be able to decrease) the size of the compensation package in order to attract an individual who would do the job equally well? Then you are probably not paying what the work is worth and should consider revising what you are paying them.

Fourth, look through a *sample personal budget*. What makes for a sustainable family budget at different stages of life in your locality? Ask this question of several people in their fifties and sixties, as those much younger may not fully understand what it really costs to raise a family, and those who are older may no longer remember. Why do this if you are paying your staff based on their work rather than on their needs? Because compensation is not a purely deductive process and you should check what you think the work is worth against a typical level of need.[5]

---

5. Three notes regarding compensation: (1) Do not assume that just because a compensation package worked for a person's predecessor it will work for them as well. Different people have

Finally, have some *honest conversations*. Ensure that someone in leadership in your church speaks regularly with your staff about how their compensation package is serving them and their families. Do they feel there is parity across staff? Are they finding their ministry hampered for want of money? Consider that feedback carefully.

WHAT ABOUT STAFF IN FINANCIAL DISTRESS?

What should a church do when its own staff are struggling financially? It is important in these situations to keep in mind the principle I outlined earlier from 1 Timothy 5, that it is a person's labor that makes them worthy of pay. Here are some questions to ask when your staff are in financial hardship:

1. Is this our fault? Has the church been underpaying for the work they receive? In that case, the church might provide a bonus to remedy this wrong in addition to adjusting compensation. A staff member's level of need is not irrelevant to this assessment: only in unusual situations (as with a trainee) should a church hire a staff member *knowing* that compensation will not be sufficient to meet their needs.

---

different needs (say, particular health issues or family they need to care for in a different country). (2) Some churches start with a benchmark and then subtract what a staff member would have given to the church, surmising that it's more tax-efficient to not pay them this in the first place. Don't do this! Since giving is one of the main purposes for income (Eph. 4:28) and pastors are to be examples to the flock (1 Pet. 5:3), don't deprive pastors of the joy of giving simply because they work for a church. (3) Even if your pastor is single, it is wise to consider needs based on the needs of a family. After all, he may one day have a family, or even if he doesn't, his replacement might. Don't pay less merely because of the marital status of your pastor.

2. Are they in the wrong job? You should not increase compensation simply because a person's needs have increased. It may be that this person's needs are simply more than this job can support. In that case you might help them upskill so they can make a transition to a different job.

3. Are finances being mismanaged? Perhaps financial distress has come because a staff member doesn't manage their money well. This may be cause for (1) questioning whether a pastor is disqualified from office by failing to "manage his own household well" (1 Tim. 3:4 ESV); and/or (2) teaching them about financial management.

4. Do they need temporary financial help? If they do, then assist them in a way that does not compromise their dignity or respect. Do be sure, however, to make it clear that this is benevolence and not compensation, as to not confuse Jesus's principle that the worker is worthy of their wages.* As is true with any use of benevolence funds, this is a good short-term solution but not a viable long-term solution.

---

* A separation between benevolence and compensation is important in your communication to them, but the two may be indecipherable for tax reasons. Most likely, benevolence to a staff member will be seen by taxing authorities as taxable income.

That short phrase in Titus 3 is remarkably powerful in summarizing these goals for compensation. "See that they lack nothing." Paying your pastor is one of the most important things your church budget can do. As such, unless your congregation really doesn't have the money, one of your top budget priorities should be to pay a pastor and to ensure that his compensation is a help to his ministry, erring on the side of generosity.

Trust

In addition to generosity, consider the importance of *trust*. Several years before I began working as a pastor at my church, I served on our church's compensation committee. I did this while working in a career in business, having no idea that the salary I was helping to set would one day be my own. I'm in the unique position of having designed a church compensation plan that I now live with! One lesson I've learned from that transition—from layman to staff pastor—is the inherent vulnerability of working for a church.

Consider, by way of analogy, the difference between working for a large corporation and working for your father's small business. Both situations involve trust—but trust in a family-run company is different because *the relationship extends beyond the business.*

When I worked in the business world, my employer expected me to look out for myself, and I negotiated my compensation with that in mind. When I began work for my church, however, the dynamic shifted. It was more like working for the family business. Of course, we discussed my compensation before I accepted the job, but not in the freewheeling way that's expected in the for-profit world. The implicit agreement, now that I work for my church, is that I will spend my energy for them—and that they will care for me. When that vulnerability is held in trust, it makes for a wonderful working relationship between a pastor and his church.

As a church, hold that trust carefully. One way you can do that if you *don't* work for a church is by understanding how your church's pay package works. Do you know the tax burdens and benefits of working as a pastor? Do you know how much your pastor's pay has increased in the last five years relative to inflation? Do you know how your church accounts for your pastor's housing (which in the US has special tax treatment)? How confident are you that staff are paid in parity with each other, accounting for merit, experience, and education? If your general response is, "those details aren't of interest to me," or "it's my pastor's job to bring up any problems with compensation," I would challenge you as to whether you fully appreciate the vulnerable place that your church staff are in.

PASTORAL PAY PRINCIPLES TO AGREE ON

The group that sets pastoral pay should agree on which compensation principles the church should be committed to. Which items in this list can/should you agree to?

- We will pay pastors such that they can support a family on this income alone.
- We will pay pastors such that they can afford to live near where our church meets.
- We will pay pastors such that they can save for retirement (if this isn't already included in the compensation benchmarks you use).
- We will pay pastors enough that they can give money away.
- We will base a pastor's total comp package on one or more suitable external benchmarks.
- We will err on the side of being generous.

Advocating for Your Own Pay

When is it appropriate for a pastor to advocate for changes in his own compensation? If a pastor is "not a lover of money" (1 Tim. 3:3), shouldn't he take whatever the church gives him without complaining? I believe a pastor should take an active role in making sure his pay package is adequate. But there are a few things to keep in mind when you (pastors) do this.

Be careful that you don't mislead your church as to how much you cost. Within the "vulnerable but safe" ethos I described above, assume your church *wants* to see that you "lack nothing." Help them do their job! Imagine you're getting ready to pastor a church. You take the job even though the pay seems low. You think to yourself, "I can make this work for now, and I'm sure we can adjust things later." But you don't make that clear when you are hired. Now, three years in, you find you need to take a second job to make ends meet, and you resent the church for not taking better care of you (which may be a valid concern). But remember: you accepted the job without complaint—and you're only now telling them that you need more money, and that you've *always* known you'll need more money. Do you see how they might feel misled?

Another factor to keep in mind if you're the main preaching pastor is that your pay package will be the basis for compensating any future staff. For their sakes, help your church come to an appropriately generous compensation philosophy. The reality is that someday you'll need to be replaced, so don't get your church accustomed to unrealistic expectations in how much they need to pay a pastor. If they pay you more than you need, just quietly give it back!

How then should you talk about your own pay? Not in the context of negotiation, but in the context of trust, with the purpose of providing accurate information. You might say something like this: "To be honest, that figure isn't going to work for my family in the long term. For the next year or so, my wife can get a job and we will gladly make this work. But if I'm going to be here long term, which I'd really like, we'll eventually need to move toward a figure more like $XX,XXX. Otherwise, you'll need to find a less expensive pastor." Be sure to consider any additional factors that might influence your compensation, like experience or the size of the church. Keep in mind that if you're young and inexperienced, you probably don't deserve the pay package your predecessor had. Here are four suggestions for talking with your church about your compensation:

1. *Keep the conversation private.* Ideally this conversation is between you and a designated leader in your church—perhaps the chair of your compensation committee or the chair of your

session. More generally, it's wise for the church to have one lay leader as the point person on all matters of compensation (ideally a nonstaff pastor/elder). This way, one person in authority will accept full responsibility for these issues without holding any personal bias.

2. *Your goal is to provide information, not to negotiate.* Unless you're really at the point where finances might force you out of the job, don't pretend that they'll lose you if they don't boost your pay.

3. *Assume they want what you want.* Many churches desire to pay their pastors generously, in line with Scriptural admonitions. Before you accuse them of being too stingy, ask them about their objectives for your compensation. You may be surprised to discover that you're all working for the same goal, even if there is disagreement on how to get there.

4. *Don't make them do all the work.* Work through your personal budget, complete with ministerial tax implications, and humbly ask for their feedback on your expectations and lifestyle.

Conclusion: Making Vulnerability Safe

What's the goal in setting staff pay? The goal is to make the vulnerable relationship between a church and its staff feel safe for your staff. You want to ensure their ministry is not hampered by financial concerns. And you want to equip your congregation for works of service. In all this, staff are a means to an end: God-glorifying ministry in the church. This brings us to the next section of your budget: church programs and ministries.

PROGRAMS

*Equipping the Congregation
for Ministry*

What programs or ministries should your church budget include? Children's ministry, music ministry, women's ministry, mercy ministry . . . the options seem endless. Because these ministries so closely affect the lives of your congregation, prioritizing them can be a challenge.

"With all these kids entering their teen years, funding youth ministry should be our top priority."

"Eliminate the Moms of Preschoolers program? You can't possibly do that!"

"Cut the music budget? But that's what first brought me to this church!"

You get the picture. How do you decide which ministries to fund?

Funding What Is Faithful

The answer to that question brings us back to the goal we talked about in chapter one: faithfulness to the Great Commission. Let's presume that every program in your church budget falls inside that command: to make more and better disciples. How do you prioritize? How do you determine which programs are the *most* faithful to the Great

Commission? That requires a deeper unpacking of what faithfulness means for your church.

Remember the vision of faithfulness we saw in the parable of the talents: actions are faithful when they show off the goodness and glory of the Master. How does a church do that? Consider the model of Ephesians 2–3. There, Paul describes a group of sinful Jews and sinful gentiles with little in common except for a centuries-long history of animosity. Bring them together into the local church where they rub shoulders together and deal with each other's sin and have hard conversations and make difficult decisions together. Things explode, right? Well, no. Having exulted in their salvation (Eph. 1:1–2:10), Paul describes a supernatural unity that existed among Jews and gentiles in the local church at Ephesus because of that salvation.

Why is that unity important? The answer is in Ephesians 3:10: "His intent was that now, through the church, the manifold wisdom of God should be made known to the rulers and authorities in the heavenly realms." Even the heavens above stare in wonder at God's wisdom showcased by unity in the church. And what is it in a church that provokes such wonder? Two items in particular.

First, it is the *breadth* of our commitment to each other. In Ephesians, Paul is writing about the amazing reality that the church includes the natural enemies of Jew and gentile (2:18). Similarly, your church reveals the glory of God when it reaches across societal boundaries of age, ethnicity, race, personality, status, politics, and so forth.[1] Second, along with that, Paul describes *depth* of commitment: in Christ, Jew and gentile are even more committed than family (2:19). Your church reveals the glory of God when diverse followers of Christ have a depth of commitment to one another far beyond their own self-

---

1. It should be noted that the Jew-gentile dynamic in the early church is not entirely analogous to diversity in our own churches since the old covenant separation of Jew and gentile had been theological as well as ethnic and political. Yet this discontinuity notwithstanding, Ephesians 2–3 still shows the value of unity amidst natural enemies. Acts 6, addressed elsewhere in this book, considers matters of unity and diversity that are more similar to what our churches face today.

interest. This kind of love defies naturalistic explanations. It's a giant arrow pointing to the power of almighty God.

More Attractive than the Attractional Church

This awe-inspiring breadth and depth of community are central to God's purpose for every church. That means we can evaluate ministries and programs by their ability to fuel a breadth and depth of community that evidences God's supernatural work in our hearts.

To see how this works out practically, let's contrast this way of evaluating a ministry with a different vision for church programs, one that is often called the "attractional" church. In this ministry paradigm, the goal of a church is to attract as many people as possible. You want to attract non-Christians so they can hear the gospel. You want to attract unchurched Christians so they can grow in their faith. You attract these people by designing programs and ministries that meet those felt needs. Then as they come into your church, good gospel work happens. In that mind-set, you evaluate programs and ministries for how effective they are in attracting and integrating newcomers.

Do you see the difference between the "faithfulness-focused" church and this "attraction-focused" church I just described? Both of these churches are eager to obey the Great Commission, and amidst any criticism I may offer, let's commend that motivation. But they have *different definitions of success*. The attraction-focused church evaluates success of a ministry based on the size of the crowd it draws. In contrast, the faithfulness-focused church evaluates success based on the kind of community it grows.

These two different visions for church are behind many debates about which ministries and programs a church should fund. At the risk of making a caricature, let me briefly draw out some implications of these competing visions for the dimensions of depth and breadth I described earlier.

Depth (Consumers vs. Providers)

The attractional church treats people as consumers and advertises itself as a place to meet their needs. Not surprisingly, people commit to the church as they see best meeting those needs. The problem with this vision is that the Bible treats Christians not as consumers but as providers: "We love because he first loved us" (1 John 4:19). Biblical commitment to a local church is rooted not in what we can get but in what we've been given in Christ. Commitment in a consumer-oriented church can be explained entirely by natural laws of human behavior. On the other hand, in a faithfulness-focused church, when commitment goes deeper than self-interest, it points to the supernatural power of the gospel.

Breadth (Similarity vs. Diversity)

The programs that consumers find attractive are generally built around similarity: similarity of need, similarity of stage of life, similarity of interest. After all, that's the power of niche marketing: ministry aimed at a homogeneous group of people is more likely to meet their needs. Ministry built on similarity is comfortable and familiar.

Yet nothing about this testifies to God's power. Rich people gravitate to rich people, Asians to Asians, the educated to the educated, teachers to teachers, regardless of whether they're indwelt by the Spirit. Similarity says much about a love for the familiar; it says little about God or the gospel. In contrast, the New Testament's vision is quite different: a church characterized by deep love between those who have little in common other than Christ. Jew and gentile (Eph. 3), rich and poor (James 2), widows and families (Acts 6), and young and old (Titus 2) are just some of the groups Christ bonds together. As Jesus said in Luke 6:32, "If you love those who love you, what credit is that to you? Even sinners love those who love them." How does a love of similarity testify to the gospel's power?

What's ironic is that in the long run, a church centered on faithfulness is profoundly more attractive than an attractional church. The attractional church uses consumerism and similarity to appeal to its audience using tools that are little different from any other market-driven organization. The faithfulness-focused church, on the other hand, builds a community of depth and breadth that could never exist except for the truth and power of a supernatural gospel. Because it depends on commitment to Christ rather than commitment to comfort, it extends to those with whom we share little in common other than Christ. The result? A church that is supernaturally attractive. "By this everyone will know that you are my disciples, if you love one another" (John 13:35).[2]

With this as a foundation, we can use these two dimensions of community to evaluate a budget's programs and ministries. First, do your programs encourage people to act as consumers or providers (depth)? Second, do they encourage similarity or diversity (breadth)? Don't kill a ministry simply because it's grounded in similarity or just because it meets felt needs. But be wary of what this might mean for the health of a ministry and what it says about God and the gospel. Recognize a program's potential to create community in your church that's entirely naturalistic rather than community that demands a supernatural explanation.

Let's examine the impact of church programs on depth and breadth of community, taking each in turn.

Consumers or Providers?

Let's start with depth of community. Do your programs treat people as consumers or providers? To better frame that question, let's look back to Ephesians. In chapter 4, Paul explains how the heaven-provoking church of chapter 3 equips Christians to be spiritual providers. "Christ himself gave the apostles, the prophets, the evangelists, the pastors and teachers, to equip his people for works of service, so that the body of

---

2. This concept of church community with supernatural depth and breadth is explored more fully in *The Compelling Community: Where God's Power Makes a Church Attractive* by Mark Dever and Jamie Dunlop (Wheaton: Crossway, 2015).

Christ may be built up" (vv. 11–12). What do all these people in verse 11 have in common? They are all ministers of the Word. And note that they aren't *doing* ministry; they're equipping the congregation to be ministers (v. 12). And that congregational ministry bears some amazing fruit! It bears unity and maturity in Christ (v. 13), and orthodoxy and stability of doctrine (v. 14).

Your church's programs and ministries can help you do this well by facilitating either the ministry of teaching (v. 11) or the ministry of the congregation (v. 12).

Ministry of Teaching

Some programs are designed to help the teaching ministry of the church. For example, a key goal of children's ministry is to help parents remain undistracted in the service so they can be better disciples of Christ and disciplers of their kids. The sound ministry helps the congregation hear the sermon. The music ministry is itself a form of teaching as we sing great truths of Scripture to God and to each other.

Here's an important question: For the programs at your church that are in the teaching category, how effectively are they doing this? If they've expanded to pursue additional priorities, how well are they serving this most essential purpose? For example, in addition to providing childcare, your children's ministry may also teach gospel truths to the kids, forge connections between caregivers and families, equip families to teach their kids, and make church a fun place for everyone. But perhaps those goals have made the ministry so large and complex that a significant number of parents now spend their Sundays in children's ministry instead of being equipped by good teaching. In that case, it's time to consider a simpler program that better accomplishes its original purpose.

Ministry of the Congregation

The good things Paul mentions in Ephesians 4 (unity, maturity, orthodoxy, stability) don't come directly from solid teaching. They come as the saints, equipped by that teaching, engage in the work of ministry. Here, too, church programs can help as they facilitate congregational ministry. Yet two design flaws can impede a program's ability to do this well.

First, programs may actually distract your congregation from those areas of ministry that are most valuable. Of course, what constitutes "valuable" congregational ministry is quite subjective. But Ephesians 4 offers a good guidepost. The main type of ministry Paul has in mind in Ephesians 4 seems to be relational ministry: "Speaking the truth in love, we will grow to become in every respect the mature body of him who is the head, that is, Christ" (v. 15).

Look through the programs and ministries listed in your budget that you feel fall into this category of facilitating congregational ministry. Which ones offer the least relational return on the time, stress, and enthusiasm your congregation invests? Consider that the inner workings of your church can offer more than sufficient cover for a works-oriented person to take shelter from the gospel. Someone can think they are doing great with God because of all the time they volunteer at church without ever meeting 1 John's criteria of loving their brother or sister (4:8).

If ministries in your church seem like they're a poor use of your congregation's time, you may want to reprogram them or eventually defund them altogether. If you think an individual sees the church as being mainly about programs rather than about people, you might suggest they step back from their formal area of service for a time to focus better on the more essential, informal ministry of loving others in the church.

A second design flaw is that a program can feed into the idea that church is "all about meeting my needs." This can be especially prevalent when staff are evaluated based on how big a crowd they can draw—encouraging them to appeal to people as consumers. When the goals of a program or ministry are geared toward meeting felt needs, it can fuel an attitude of consumeristic entitlement. But it's important to recognize that people can become entitled not only with being served but also with serving, when they feel that the goal of a certain program is to give them the opportunity to use their gifts and help them feel "fulfilled" in ministry. Contrary to that, the apostle Paul wrote that gifts are given not for personal fulfillment, but for the edification of the church (1 Cor. 14:12).

HOW TO GENTLY END A BAD PROGRAM

How can you direct congregational effort away from a program or ministry that's a poor use of their time without causing unnecessary damage? Here are four strategies to consider:

1. Use times of financial constraint. When the budget needs to be trimmed, seek to weed out those sections of the budget that seem to be the least valuable for your congregation.
2. Use new spending opportunities. When your congregation is excited about a new budget item (perhaps sending out one of their own as a missionary), you might eliminate poorly designed programs as a way to make space in the budget.
3. Use the departure of a leader. Often when a ministry leader leaves, it's sometimes up to the pastor to find a replacement. That can be an opportunity to sunset a ministry instead of identifying a new leader.
4. Redesign a program. Often the best answer is to work with the leaders of a particular ministry to change its shape and purpose into something that better serves God's purpose for your church.

As an example of both these obstacles, take the experience of a friend of mine who served as the director of a men's ministry at his church. Having taken the job, he soon realized he was essentially an events coordinator, and the church was evaluating his job performance based on how many men he could get to attend the events. Much time and money went into pulling off events to incorporate men into the life of the church—but many still didn't know each other very well. My friend felt he was hosting events for the sake of hosting events (design flaw #1). Beyond that, you can see how that kind of ministry becomes very consumer-oriented. Figure out what men want and design events that meet their preferences (design flaw #2). So my friend went to the elders and asked if he could change the ministry's vision from an event-driven ministry to a discipling-driven ministry. They approved, and he stopped doing most of the events. Now his job was clear: to equip men to meet together throughout the week to encourage one another in their spiritual lives. This item in the church budget is now more closely aligned with the priorities of Scripture, with (we pray) more spiritual fruit as a result.

Similarity or Diversity?

This men's ministry example demonstrates an evaluation of programs based on *depth* of commitment. But what about the *breadth* of community we saw in Ephesians 2–3?

Envision a church where customized programs serve each segment of the congregation. Youth, students, young adults, young families, mid-career professionals, and retirees all have their own ministries, be they classes, small groups, breakfasts, or play groups. By some measures, you get a very tight-knit congregation: it's easy to build community where people share much in common. But now instead of having one congregation, you have several. The church may look diverse from the outside, but in reality it's a loose collection of homogeneous clusters. Is that the kind of unity that makes the heavens stare in wonder (Eph. 3:10)?

Our old nature is to value comfort more than Christ. And as comfort-seeking people, we gravitate toward relationships where we share much in common. But as a Christian, in your new nature, you should value Christ over comfort. You'll still benefit from relationships where you enjoy similarity. But leaning into your new nature, you'll also build friendships where you share little in common but Christ. Over time, that will become easier and those kinds of friendships will become a source of great joy.

Let's see how all this applies to church programs, taking a church singles ministry as an example. There is real spiritual value in ministering to single adults. But most likely the singles in your church are spending time together regardless of whether you have a singles ministry. In general, church programs should help members lean into their new nature, which values Christ more than comfort, rather than simply appealing to them on the basis of their old nature, which seeks comfort. Doing that might mean phasing out the singles ministry. Or it might mean recommissioning it to encourage relationships between singles and the rest of the church.

Imagine a youth ministry focused on connecting families and young adults, where the young adults mentor the youth and learn from the families. Imagine a student ministry designed to integrate the lives of older adults and students—a bridge between the campus and the church. Imagine a Moms of Preschoolers group designed to help young moms build friendships with retirees. The possibilities are endless.

The great news here is that relationships that stretch beyond what's comfortable have the potential to be some of the deepest, most satisfying friendships. Imagine, for example, a friendship I have with a fellow Chicago Cubs fan in my church. What do we talk about? Jesus, of course. And the Cubs. A lot about the Cubs. Now, take a different friendship. We're both Christians, but we really have to scratch our heads to think of anything else we share in common. What do we talk about? Jesus. After all, what else *can* we talk about? Now, which is a better foundation for a friendship: the Chicago Cubs or Jesus? You get the picture. Friendships that lean into your new, Christ-loving nature will take longer to form and they'll require more charity and more patience, but they are a gold mine of joy and praise.

Programs that feed into similarity aren't necessarily bad—they just have a downside that we often don't appreciate.[3] Your job as a church leader is to review the costs and benefits of each program in the budget. Sometimes it's worth the downside to unity to fund a program that serves just a segment of your congregation. But where possible, encourage programs aimed at the whole congregation and that trade on the glory of unity rather than the comfort of similarity.

A Regulated, Free-Market Approach to Funding Programs

Let's say your church has the goals I've just described: programs that equip people as spiritual providers; programs that facilitate unity. You may make some exceptions here and there, but by and large, those are your goals.

How do you decide which ministries to fund? Do you invite grant proposals from the congregation? Fund whatever you funded last year? Just ask the pastor? Let me offer a funding philosophy that I hope you'll find to be as useful as it has been for my church. First, let's contrast two different extremes in how churches might decide which programs to fund.

The Top-Down Approach

In this model, programs flow down from church leadership and staff. As a leadership team, you determine where the most fruitful places will be for your congregants to invest their time. You do that based on your history as a church, feedback you get from your members, and your own wisdom as a pastoral team. However, this is hardly the "*equip* the saints for the work of the ministry" mentality of Ephesians 4, is it? It's more like "*tell* the saints what to do"—feeding them into your menu of predetermined options.

---

3. Dever and Dunlop, *The Compelling Community*, 79.

The Bottom-Up Approach

The alternative isn't much more appealing though. In this case the leadership of the church focuses its effort exclusively on teaching God's Word. You teach about the importance of loving each other, loving your neighbors, of the priority of gospel proclamation—and pray that your people will apply these truths well. This has the advantage of providing great freedom for congregational initiative. But wouldn't they benefit from the wisdom and experience of their leaders in determining where to focus? And unless you're in a very small church, coordinating ministry between church members is going to be a real challenge without any central organization.

A Third Way: Reactive, But Not Passive

As you probably guessed, I'm going to propose an alternative, the "best of both worlds" approach. In this model, we lead with the preaching of the Word. Then as church leaders, we watch to see where that Word is taking root and flowering into action. We respond by using church resources to support the most promising of those ideas. Those resources could include coordination of volunteer resources through a weekly prayer meeting, social media, or an online bulletin board, highlighting member initiatives in sermon application or preservice announcements, creating diaconal positions, and yes, even using money in the church budget.

In this model, church leadership is reactive. They react to what church members initiate. But they aren't passive: they actively promote the most promising member-prompted ideas. As I've described elsewhere, you might think of this as a regulated, free-market approach.[4] On the one hand, it's a free market. Rather than telling people how to live out the Christian life (as the top-down approach can do), we watch to see what naturally takes shape as the Spirit convicts through the Word. Yet this is not wild frontier capitalism. We deliberately help

---

4. Mark Dever and Jamie Dunlop, *The Compelling Community: Where God's Power Makes a Church Attractive* (Wheaton: Crossway, 2015), 194.

the best ideas to prosper and unapologetically use the resources of the church to do so.

If interest wanes and members focus their effort away from a certain ministry, the church will slowly reallocate its resources in response. At times, you may rescue a program you feel is undervalued by the congregation. But in general, when the congregation abandons a program, you let it die. Don't underestimate the great collective wisdom resident in a congregation of Spirit-filled believers all seeking to determine how best to serve God with limited time and resources.

Very often, it will take some backbone to let a program die or to say no to a suboptimal new program. I remember a situation when I should have had more of a backbone: a brand-new Christian came up with an idea for raising money for a worthy ministry in our neighborhood. It seemed clear to me that the amount of money raised would hardly justify the many hours of volunteer time it would take to pull this off. But I didn't want to discourage her, so I gave her a green light. Not surprisingly, the congregation saw better ways to use their time and didn't volunteer to help out. This dear sister came to me looking for help, but I wasn't about to sell an idea I didn't believe in to a congregation who didn't believe in it either. She was deeply discouraged—much more so than if I'd simply been honest and better channeled her enthusiasm in the first place.

More positively, here are three other examples from my church's experience to give you a better sense of what this model looks like.

1. The first example is a Bible study that was held at a juvenile detention center in a nearby city. One member began the ministry, and one of our pastors helped him explain its importance to the congregation. More people began joining him, and a second study was launched. Eventually, however, the member who started the ministry left the area, and interest waned. We decided not to take any special measures to revive congregational interest, and the ministry ended.

2. My second example is a homeless shelter on the other side of our city. Our church had worked with them for a better part of a century, but fifteen years ago no one from our church was involved. We knew that this shelter was planning on moving closer to our church, however, so we kept them in our budget, made sure our pastors got to know their leaders better, and asked the congregation to pray that some of our members would discover a renewed vision to serve there. Sure enough, one member caught the vision, passed it along to others, and now we have many members there on a regular basis, tutoring residents, making food, leading Bible studies, and building friendships.

3. The last example is an English language ministry for international students at a nearby university. This ministry had been small-scale for years. Two things changed, however: it attracted new leadership, and word got around among international students that these English classes used the Bible as their primary text. Interest exploded, and soon one hundred students were involved, which meant one hundred volunteers were needed as one-on-one language partners/evangelists. The informal leadership structure began to break down, and so one of our pastors offered help. We created a deacon position to lead the ministry, gave them money from our budget, and helped them communicate this opportunity to the congregation.

In one example, the pastors let a worthy ministry end. In the second, they felt that a failing ministry was undervalued by the congregation and so they put it on life support. In the third example, they followed the congregation's lead and supported the cause with church resources.

Remember that this reactive but strategic approach only applies to programs. It would be unwise to employ this reactive approach in more fundamental areas where your church has clear commands to obey—like paying your pastor, caring for the needy in your flock, or securing a meeting place. And even among programs, those designed to facilitate teaching will more often follow a top-down model. After all, the Bible envisions teaching as a top-down enterprise (from the pastors, with accountability to the congregation, under Christ). So programs like children's ministry, music ministry, sound ministry, etc. will normally receive more direction from church leadership. On the other hand, programs designed to facilitate congregational ministry should generally follow the regulated free-market model. In these cases, leadership is important, but initiative normally emanates from the congregation.

Conclusion: Be Deliberate to Be Faithful

The programs you fund will shape your church significantly—for good or ill. So be deliberate about what you fund. As a starting point, you might use the scorecard at the end of this chapter. Note that it is less an evaluation of program success and more an evaluation of program design. After all, "success" in ministry isn't something we can measure in this life—fruit is God's work. Sometime before you begin next year's budgeting process, you might use this to structure a line-by-line review of all the programs your church is supporting. Ideally, that conversation will help you better understand which programs are most valuable, which should be pushed aside, and which could benefit from a redesign.

While programs can be a significant factor in shaping your church's internal ministry, the next chapter will focus on how your church conceives of and spends on its external ministry.

Ministry Assessment Worksheet

Download an editable copy at
https://www.9marks.org/budgetresources

Fill out the shaded area, then ask leadership team members to complete the worksheet to assess the design and objectives for a ministry/program. Discuss as part of the budget process.

Ministry name: _____ Leader(s): _____

Budget commitment last year: $_____

CONGREGATIONAL PARTICIPATION

What portion of the congregation participates in a typical month? ____%

Is participation increasing / decreasing / static? **(circle one)**

Is this ministry led by staff / deacons / other members? **(circle one)**

ASSESSMENT OF MINISTRY GOALS

What would you describe as the objective(s) of this ministry?
_____

Who are the target participants for this ministry? _____

Whom does this ministry benefit? _____

Assess the alignment of this ministry's goals with the Great Commission:

- Making Disciples   LOW ○──○──○──○▶○ HIGH
- Equipping Disciples   LOW ○──○──○──○▶○ HIGH

ASSESSMENT OF MINISTRY DESIGN

This ministry . . .	Disagree	Neutral	Agree
. . . appeals to participants by seeking to meet their needs.	○	○	○
. . . equips people to be spiritual providers.	○	○	○
. . . serves the whole of our church.	○	○	○
. . . connects types of people who ordinarily don't spend time together.	○	○	○

How well does the congregation perceive the spiritual value of this ministry? overestimate / rightly-estimate / underestimate **(circle one)**?

MISSIONS AND OUTREACH

Becoming a Discriminating Investor

Dorothy Vogel was a librarian; her husband, Herb, was a postal worker. Yet together they assembled one of the most important art collections of the twentieth century, worth millions of dollars. How did they do it?

With great love for art but little money to spend, the Vogels passed over the art establishment and focused instead on emerging artists near their Manhattan home. They bought what they liked, and their tastes proved perceptive; artists they bought from often hit it big. Eventually, being acquired by the Vogels became a badge of honor, and that made for some unbelievable bargains. As one artist suggested to a friend when he learned Herb and Dorothy were interested in his work: "Take off three zeros and cut the price in half."[1] Early in his career, the legendary Christo sold them his work in exchange for cat-sitting services. Eventually, nearly five thousand works of art filled the couple's

---

1. Matt Schudel, "Herbert Vogel, unlikely art collector and benefactor of National Gallery, dies at 89," July 22, 2012, *The Washington Post*, https://www.washingtonpost.com/local/obituaries/herbert-vogel-unlikely-art-collector-and-benefactor-of-national-gallery-dies-at-89/2012/07/22/gJQANqOf2W_story.html?noredirect=on&utm_term=.d45a2b13bb4d.

one-bedroom apartment, along with eight cats and twenty exotic turtles. Grappling with space constraints, they donated their collection in 1992 to the National Gallery in Washington, DC, where they had honeymooned thirty years earlier. Today their names are engraved in stone at the museum's entrance.

Investing for Eternal Value

Why do I share this story? Because I think there are some important similarities between your church's outreach budget and Herb and Dorothy's long-sighted purchases. Like them, you're sorting through investment opportunities to find what in the long run will prove to be priceless. Only instead of buying art, you're investing in international missions, church planting, pastor training, and so forth—which collectively I'm calling "outreach." And whereas their investment horizon spanned a lifetime, your focus is on what will prove valuable in eternity.

The stakes are high. Not everything labeled "outreach" will prove to be of lasting value. Consider this warning from the apostle Paul in 1 Corinthians 3:12–15 about the value of church-planting work: "If anyone builds on this foundation [of Christ] using gold, silver, costly stones, wood, hay or straw, their work will be shown for what it is, because the Day will bring it to light. It will be revealed with fire, and the fire will test the quality of each person's work. If what has been built survives, the builder will receive a reward. If it is burned up, the builder will suffer loss but yet will be saved—even though only as one escaping through the flames."

As you assemble your church budget, you're accepting responsibility to sort gold, silver, and costly stones from the wood, hay, and straw. Are you up to the task? I'll argue in this chapter that you *can* be up to the task if you pay attention to Jesus's investing advice: invest in the local church.

Framing the Challenge

Before we get to Jesus's advice, we need to examine two basic challenges you'll face in assembling your outreach budget: measuring impact and the difficulty of funding from a distance.

Measuring Impact

In recent decades, the measurement of impact has become commonplace in the world of philanthropy. This is good for donors: it helps them know what their money is accomplishing. And it's good for nonprofits: it helps them direct effort to the highest-impact opportunities. As wonderful as this mentality is, however, it hits a major roadblock with gospel work: we can't always measure the impact of gospel work. In fact, sometimes attempts to measure gospel work can damage it quite severely.

You can measure inputs to gospel work (for example, how many people your missionaries shared the gospel with, how many friendships with non-Christians they developed, how much time they give to teaching new Christians). You can see evidence of impact (e.g., number of churches meeting, spiritual fruit, changed lives). Yet you cannot measure the actual impact of the work itself, unlike your ability to measure other types of philanthropy, like how many children were fed, how fast malaria infection rates decreased, or reductions in poverty rates.

For example, you don't know how many people truly came to Christ through a missionary's ministry; only God knows. What's more, faithful inputs don't always translate to impressive results because results are up to God. Consider the prophet Ezekiel's experience: God called him to preach faithfully (Ezek. 2:5) but *promised* that the people of Israel would not listen (Ezek. 3:7). This is one key difference between philanthropy in general and your church's desire to fund the Great Commission.

Fortunately, God doesn't measure success based on impact but on faithfulness (though as you'll recall from chapter one, the two are normally related). And that brings us to a second challenge.

Funding from a Distance

Unlike Herb and Dorothy, who lived in the same city as the artists they were investing in, much of your outreach budget is funding people and projects that aren't nearby. It's not easy to understand a ministry that's halfway around the world—and monthly newsletters can't tell the whole story. Even ministries closer at hand can be difficult to know well.

Let's say you support the Maple Street Mission across town because several of your members have been involved there for years. How discerning are those members? Are they in a position to ask good questions about ministry methods and Great Commission faithfulness?

My concern is not so much people who fraudulently enrich themselves with your outreach money—though I'm sure that can happen. My concern is gospel work that honestly conceives of itself as valuable—and yet in the end will amount to nothing of lasting value. For example:

- Ministries built on evangelistic methods that produce thousands of "converts" in name only—most of whom are not walking with Jesus years or even months later.
- Missionaries who spend nearly all their time and energy just surviving in a difficult place but do not devote much time to real gospel work.
- Partnerships with ministries that promote the prosperity gospel. What's advertised as genuine gospel work is nothing more than selling God as the source of guaranteed health, wealth, and happiness.

- Organizations that, while having a Christian history, now scoff at historic Christian beliefs—like the exclusivity of Jesus Christ for salvation, or commitment to salvation through faith alone—yet still use a historic statement of beliefs to raise funds from Bible-believing Christians.

Investing from a distance would be just fine, so long as you could objectively measure the ministry impact of those investments. We do this all the time, for example in the stock market. But investing from a distance when impact is *difficult* to measure (at least by us humans) makes for a real challenge. In view of these difficulties, let me offer up five pieces of advice as your church goes about assembling the outreach section of its budget.

1. Fund the Local Church

Benjamin Franklin is famous for saying that nothing in this world is certain except death and taxes.[2] Had Franklin been a Christian, he might have added a third: the local church. After all, no other institution on earth has Jesus's promise of permanence: "I will build my church, and the gates of Hades will not overcome it" (Matt. 16:18). Jesus obviously didn't say that *your* church is invincible. But the local church as an institution will prevail, until time stands still.

It's like God whispering in your ear in 1890, "invest in the automobile" or in 1990, "invest in the internet." "Of all the trends out there, this one will last!" Jesus's promise won't answer all our questions about outreach funding, but it sure gets us a long way!

If you want to invest in what will last, invest in the local church. That doesn't mean every check should name a specific church in the

2. Letter to Jean-Baptiste Leroy, 1789: "Our new Constitution is now established, and has an appearance that promises permanency; but in this world nothing can be said to be certain, except death and taxes."

"pay to" line. But in general, each item in your outreach budget should have a strong connection to the health of the local church. I'll walk through several outreach items that churches commonly fund and give examples.

Church planting among the unreached. Your church may be using money to help start new churches where the gospel is not known. You'll notice that the label I use is "church planting" and not simply "evangelism." In a place where the gospel is new news, church planting certainly must start with evangelism. But in view of Jesus's focus on the local church, direct your efforts toward work that has its ultimate aim in the establishment of healthy local churches who themselves aspire to plant churches. That means that the gospel workers you support must be equipped for more than evangelism. As a team, they must have the desire, skills, and experience to eventually gather converts into healthy churches that are ably pastored. Surely your desire is not simply to see some people saved but for the gospel to take root in a place for generations to come. The church is God's chosen instrument for that kind of a movement.

Church planting among the reached. You may also be funding church planting where Christians already live, perhaps in your own area. Do those workers understand what it would look like for the church they're planting to be healthy? A church planter friend lamented to me once that his church planting training focused on how to get a church established—a few months of work—rather than how to pastor it to health—many years of work. Ensure that any evangelism efforts you fund are either connected to an existing healthy church or helping to create new ones.

For example, my church spends a significant amount of money each year supporting a student ministry overseas in a closed country that nonetheless has an indigenous gospel witness. We've been careful to articulate why *we* should be the ones funding that work and what the ministry's connection is to the local church. Our answer in this case is that the local churches in the area, being new and relatively immature, aren't yet ready to fund this work—and the student work is raising up leaders for those churches. But our desire is to one day hand that work off to the local churches.

Student work. Speaking of student work, this is another common area of outreach spending. Sometimes organizations that do this work can be wonderful partners for your church. Others function instead as church replacements—which is unhelpful for both them and their students. I remember a student group that shifted its weekly meeting to be on Sundays at 10:00 a.m. Not a good indication that they valued the local church! Look for student groups that are eager to help students get involved in your church and who are eager for nonstudent members at your church to get involved with students. Then, by partnering with them, help them further appreciate and promote the local church in the lives of students.

Teaching ministries. Many organizations are designed to help and equip Christians. These Christian organizations might help with ministry to children, counseling, finances . . . the list is endless. Once again, let the local church be your focal point. Do these organizations desire to partner with churches, or do they seem oblivious to that priority? Do they in effect enable Christians to survive *without* being in good churches? That kind of ministry might be beneficial in the short term (because they feed God's Word to Christians who are starving for it). But by helping to perpetuate an unhealthy situation, they may actually cause more harm than good in the long run. Focus your support on organizations where it's easy to explain how their work strengthens local churches.

Short-term mission trips. Short-term mission trips have exploded in popularity in recent decades but can be notorious for wasted time and money, not to mention a distraction from long-term work.[3] A study showed, for example, that US teams rushing to rebuild houses

___

3. One oft-cited statistic is that there were 120,000 American short-term missionaries in 1989 and 2.2 million in 2006. From Steve Corbett and Brian Fikkert, *When Helping Hurts: How to Alleviate Poverty Without Hurting the Poor . . . and Yourself* (Chicago: Moody, 2012), 151.

in the aftermath of a deadly hurricane spent on average $30,000 per house; the work would have cost locals about $3,000 per house.[4] If you fund short-term trips, how can you ensure they are helping rather than hurting?

Build your trips around the needs of long-term church planting workers whom you know and trust. Ask them if there is useful work they need people from your church to do. Be prepared for the answer to be no or something that doesn't sound very exciting (like providing childcare for a week). Have the discipline to pursue only legitimate needs that your congregation can meet.

Mercy ministry. Like my church, yours may contribute money to organizations that serve physical needs in your area. I would encourage you to look for two things. First, a willingness to engage in close partnership with your church (which means they take your ideas and not just your money), and second, a track record of sharing the gospel message. Secular ministries can do great good and be worthy recipients of an individual Christian's money. But the church as an institution is tasked more narrowly with the Great Commission—and that usually means every item in the budget should support gospel proclamation in some way.

The suffering church. Just like the apostle Paul raised money from churches in Southern Europe to feed starving Christians in Judea, it may be appropriate for your church to help other Christians who are struggling. It seems especially appropriate to do this for Christians who are suffering specifically because of their commitment to Jesus Christ. Look for opportunities to do this under the authority and guidance of local churches on the ground—or look for international aid groups that work under the authority of local churches on the ground.

Pastor training. A final category in many outreach budgets is pastor training. This might involve grants to seminaries, tuition support for students, or money for nonseminary training. A focus on the local church means guiding support toward students who intend to be

---

4. Robert Lupton, *Toxic Charity* (San Francisco: HarperOne, 2011), 5.

pastors and toward organizations that primarily train pastors. In addition, it involves looking for organizations that have a well-developed theology of the local church. That puts inter-denominational seminaries in a strange position. After all, being interdenominational necessarily involves *not* taking a position on questions of how a church should function. Some of these institutions do a wonderful job of compensating for that weakness through strong partnerships with local churches. Either support training institutions with a strong perspective on the local church or look for institutions with strong partnerships with local churches.

BUDGETING VERSUS SPECIAL APPEALS

Sometimes churches encourage giving to the church budget *and* to a missions fund that operates outside the budget. I would encourage you to run most or all of your outreach spending through your church's budget. Why?

1. Raising money outside the budget can teach your church that outreach spending is on a different spiritual level than other investment opportunities. This may lead your church to undervalue outreach or to overvalue it.
2. Raising money outside the budget limits the ability of church leaders to lead the church in the allocation of where its money goes.
3. As a result of #2, the trust in church leaders that's necessary for a healthy church culture may be undermined. A healthy church culture is more valuable in the long run than extra money you might raise for outreach—and in fact will likely do more for outreach.

2. Fund What You Know

My second piece of advice: fund ministries your congregation and leadership know well. Not what you used to know, not what someone in your church knows (like so-and-so's grandson who became a missionary ten years ago and you haven't really heard from him since). Fund what you know. How?

People More than Projects

It's hard to get to know a project well; it's easier to get to know a person well. Find a person in ministry you know well and whom you trust, and fund what they do, following the example of the churches in Macedonia. They funded the apostle Paul when he was planting the church in Thessalonica (Phil. 4:16); they funded Paul's gift for the churches in Judea (Rom. 15:26); they even funded Paul when he was in prison (Phil. 4:10–15). Their money followed Paul wherever he went. Interestingly, when Paul encourages the churches at Rome and Corinth to support various missionaries (e.g., Phoebe in Rom. 16:1, Timothy in 1 Cor. 16:10–11), he commends the workers but says little about their work.

Where Your Congregation Is Already Involved

Just like I recommended in my "regulated free market" suggestion in the last chapter, let your money follow your congregation—especially for outreach opportunities close to home. If a significant number of your congregants are involved in a particular ministry opportunity, you'll have not only better knowledge of it but more influence as well. For ministries farther afield, you'll probably need to rely more heavily on church leaders to know the work you're funding, given the time and expense of doing that. But once you've decided to invest in a ministry, short-term trips by members of your congregation can be an effective tool for reinforcing long-term relationships with workers (with the caveats about short-term trips I mentioned earlier).

Piggyback on Another Church's Work

Perhaps you're reading this thinking, "But we're a tiny church. How can we possibly have this level of knowledge about the work we support?" Those at small churches can thank God for other churches! Find a church you trust that is involved in the kind of outreach you'd like to do and join their work. Fund their people, join their short-term trips, and ask about needs on the field you might be able to meet. You don't have to do this alone!

3. Fund to Know More

Beyond funding what you know, you can allocate money in the budget in ways that help you learn more about where your money is going.

Greater Support to Fewer Workers

Consider the difference between funding 2 percent of the work of fifty missionaries and funding 25 percent of the work of four missionaries. A support level of 2 percent hardly justifies those workers spending time answering all your questions about their ministry, much less visiting you when they're in the area. And for most churches, fifty missionaries is too many to really know the workers or their work. Keep in mind that Jesus gave the Great Commission to all of us. Even if you pick just one missionary to support and you do it well, your work has great opportunity for faithfulness. At the end of this book, in appendix C, you'll find the annual questionnaire that my church sends to all of our supported workers each year to help us know them better.

Areas of Overlap or Proximity

There are significant advantages to supporting multiple workers in the same location or who are doing the same kind of work or are ministering to the same people group. Over time, the expertise you develop enriches the advice you're able to provide. You can act as "air traffic control," pointing your supported workers to potentially fruitful partnerships. If workers are in the same location, it's easier to visit them on the field (since you can get to multiple workers in each visit). You might even have members of your church move their jobs to those same cities to be an encouragement to the work. Instead of funding work as broadly as possible (so your missions bulletin board looks like the United Nations), you could concentrate your efforts geographically so you would be able to support workers better and get to know them better.

4. Fund for Mutual Dependence

In the book of Acts, the apostle Paul self-funded his work when necessary, but his preference was to receive money from churches (1 Cor. 9:14). This kind of dependence is good for a missionary since it brings accountability, and when urgent needs arise, they know right where to turn. But dependence can go both ways. If you take my advice about providing better support to fewer missionaries, you've concentrated your kingdom investment portfolio. That makes you more dependent on the faithfulness of their work, and as a result, you're more likely to hold them accountable.

Construct your outreach budget so that your supported workers depend on you and you depend on them. Then support them with excellence. As the apostle John says, "Please send them on their way in a manner that honors God. It was for the sake of the Name that they went out, receiving no help from the pagans. We ought therefore to show hospitality to such people so that we may work together for the truth" (3 John 6–8). Be generous in your financial support. Give them the very best of your people for short-term help and long-term support. Provide well for them when they come to visit you so that they don't feel like a casual obligation but rather a treasured partner.

Do your supported workers feel that you treat them like top-flight investments? Or more like charity cases? Imagine if Jeff Bezos, founder of Amazon.com, had asked you for money back in 1994 in exchange for 1 percent of the company. You'd have been forever grateful, wouldn't you? You'd have seen it as an amazing privilege to be involved in such a special opportunity. We should have the same attitude toward the gospel servants we support.

5. Fund for the Long Haul

Pick solid investments and stick with them for the long haul—like the Macedonians did with Paul—and you're much more likely to fund work that's faithful. Here are a few ideas for turning that into reality.

Protect Outreach

Many years ago, my church started tracking the portion of our budget we gave toward international outreach, with the ambition of increasing it by an additional 1 percent of the budget every year. Eventually, our budget growth slowed and we stabilized our international outreach at a minimum of 15 percent of our budget—plus additional money for domestic church planting and local evangelism.

At my church, walling off a section of the budget has proven quite effective. Time and again, it has protected us from sacrificing relationships with long-term supported workers during years of tight budgets. Beyond that, it's helped the congregation see the priority of outreach spending.

Prioritize Theological Alignment

Much of your ability to form long-term partnerships with supported workers and organizations will depend on how similar your beliefs are about the Bible. It's notable that when the New Testament authors appeal for funds, they write about theology more than need. For example, when Paul is raising money for starving Christians in Judea, we don't hear much about the need but instead, hear beautiful language about the incarnation and the glory of God (2 Cor. 8–9).

The book of Romans, it seems, was a support-raising letter for Paul's future work in Spain (Rom. 15:24). And what do we get? A theological gem.

Different partnerships require different degrees of theological alignment. For example, you can't plant a church together unless you agree on what a church is, how it should function, what it should teach, and so forth—a very high level of agreement. On the other hand, engaging social issues—like advocating for the unborn and the oppressed—may be something your church can do with those who agree with you on far less.

Don't underestimate the importance of theological alignment. Just because a ministry leader is a good friend of your pastor doesn't mean that there is sufficient theological alignment for a long-term partnership. All too often, churches prioritize personal relationships without fully considering what people believe, and the end result is rarely good. Pay close attention to theological issues as you pick your outreach partners, and you will likely have partners you can invest in for a very long time.

Put Your Pastors in Charge

Investing for the long haul makes for some difficult pastoral decisions. If you're going to support just a few workers, whom should you pick? How should you balance outreach opportunities with opportunities to invest in your own church? What level of theological alignment do you need for a ministry partnership? When should a missionary come home?

A missions committee may be able to offer some assistance in these matters—but ultimately these questions are for the pastors in your church. If you want to make long-term investments, your pastoral team must give time and attention to the outreach section of the budget. They'll build close relationships with those you're supporting—if possible, making regular visits to them in their place of ministry. They'll deliberate carefully over which workers should be included in the budget. And they'll invest time to support these workers in the good they're doing.

Pray

One final thought: perhaps more than any other section of the budget, the outreach section is a useful prayer guide. Remember Jesus's words "apart from me you can do nothing" (John 15:5). The best selection and support in the world accomplishes nothing if God does not do the work. So take a look through the outreach section of your budget. Does your congregation pray together for each of these items on a regular basis? Can a ministry possibly be worthy of your congregation's money but not their time in prayer? Beyond that, consider taking one morning each week to pray through this section of the budget. As you consider the ambitions that are attached to each item on that list, pray that God would do everything you hope for—and more. Paul's prayer for the Thessalonians is a great model in this regard: "We constantly pray for you, that our God may make you worthy of his calling, and that by his power he may bring to fruition your every desire for goodness and your every deed prompted by faith" (2 Thess. 1:11). May we take as much care in prayer over the budget as we do in drafting it and giving to it.

Putting These Principles to Work

I've covered a lot in this chapter; to help you put it all together, I've condensed many of these principles into a "scorecard" that you'll find at the end of this chapter. For many churches, these principles will naturally weave into conversations about outreach, and scorecards like this will be superfluous. But for others, getting some of these ideas down on paper for each item in your outreach budget will be useful and clarifying. Keep in mind that these scores and comparisons are best used as the basis for conversation and judgment; you'd be unwise to base selection entirely or even primarily on these numbers.

Conclusion: Dependent on God's Word

At the age of twenty-three, I met with a Fortune 500 CEO to explain data that I claimed revealed tens of millions of dollars in bad investments by his company. His skeptical questions rained down, and I felt completely exposed. I had no personal credibility, no industry expertise, no business experience. All I could do was cling to my data.

We should feel similarly as we look at the outreach sections of our church budgets. Left to our own wisdom, we will struggle to know which investments will prove sound from the perspective of heaven. We will struggle to predict the long-term implications of our decisions. So we cling to God's Word, knowing that he has given us everything we need for life and godliness. Listen carefully to how Scripture describes faithful gospel work and look for opportunities that align closely with those priorities.[5] Listen to Scripture and support those workers with excellence. Listen to Scripture and pray faithfully. Then wait expectantly for that Last Day when we will all glory in what God chose to do with that work.

So far, we've traveled through nearly all aspects of your church budget: staff, programs, outreach. That leaves us with one last stop: church operations. It's easy to see how faithfulness to the Great Commission closely ties to areas like missions and outreach. But what about administration and facilities? That's our next chapter.

---

5. For an excellent guide to Scripture's teaching about international missions work, see Andy Johnson, *Missions: How the Local Church Goes Global* (Wheaton: Crossway, 2017).

Missions/Outreach Scorecard

Download an editable copy of this form at
https://www.9marks.org/budgetresources.

INSTRUCTIONS

This section condenses this chapter's principles into a scorecard.
Clearly, no supported worker or ministry can be condensed into a
number. For example, if you don't agree on the gospel, you probably
shouldn't fund an opportunity, regardless of what other scores it might
get. Instead, this worksheet can help you ask the right questions about
the items in your outreach budget. You might follow these steps:

1. Have those who know each ministry best fill out the scorecard, one scorecard for each item in your outreach budget. For
   each question in the scorecard, evaluate your agreement with
   each statement on a scale of 1 to 5, with 1 = "don't agree" and
   5 = "strongly agree." If one statement doesn't seem important or
   relevant for a particular opportunity, just cross it out.
2. If you find it useful to summarize this information numerically, you
   might consider filling out a chart like the one below.
   - Calculate the average of the nonshaded lines for each cat-
     egory (People, Work, etc.) and list it in the relevant box.
     For example, for J & G Smith, the average "People" score
     is the average of 5, 4, 5, 4, and 4 = 4.4. For the "Doctrinal
     Alignment" category, however, average just those items that
     were not crossed out (5, 5, 4, and 4 = 4.5).
   - For each opportunity, take the average of the shaded boxes
     on the scorecard and list it as the "Knowledge" score next to
     that opportunity. For the example shown, this is the average
     of 5, 4, 4, 4, and 2 = 3.8.

Budget Item	People	Work	Doctrine	Method	Fit	Knowledge
J. & G. Smith	4.4	4.3	4.5	4.7	3.7	3.8
Urban Mission	4.3	3.1	2.0	2.7	3.7	1.7
D. Rodriguez	5.0	4.0	3.3	4.5	3.0	4.4

Sample Missions/Outreach Scorecard

Download an editable copy at https://www.9marks.org/budgetresources

Individual or ministry name: *J. & G. Smith*
Amount requested for budget year: *$10,000*
Church point person: *Richi Brown*

PEOPLE (if supporting an organization, leadership of that organization)

Could serve as a lay leader in our church.	5
We would happily hire as a pastor in our church.	4
Faithful in taking advantage of opportunities for ministry.	5
Personal ministry is accompanied by evident fruitfulness.	4
This person is a leader/influencer of others.	4
As a church, we know this person well (life, doctrine).	5

WORK

Work has clear connection to the Great Commission.	5
Work is about establishing/strengthening the local church.	5
High potential for this work to be an example for others.	3
I can answer these questions with confidence.	4

DOCTRINAL ALIGNMENT

We agree on how a person becomes a Christian (gospel, conversion).	5
This person could sign our church's doctrinal statement.	5
We agree on how a local church should function.	4
~~We would be excited for this person to preach in our church.~~	
We affirm this person/organization's selection of ministry partners.	4
I can answer these questions with confidence.	4

METHODOLOGICAL ALIGNMENT

We agree on how to evaluate success (speed, faithfulness, etc.)	5
We affirm the work's vision/plan/strategy.	4
We affirm leadership's trade-off between desired speed and quality.	5
I can answer these questions with confidence.	4

FIT

Work benefits from our unique skills, knowledge, relationships.	4
Our church's ministry benefits from what we learn in this partnership.	2
Our senior pastor is excited about this work.	5
I can answer these questions with confidence.	2

CHAPTER SEVEN

OPERATIONS

*Helping the Church
Proclaim and Portray*

Harvard Business School's Clayton Christensen challenges would-be innovators to consider what "job" their product performs. For example, what's the job of a milkshake? "To taste good," you might think. But observe milkshake customers, and you might answer that question differently.

As it turns out, half of all milkshakes are purchased in the early morning and are rarely consumed at a restaurant. Why? Beyond taste or nutritional value, customers are looking for a way to make a long commute more interesting. That's the job they hire the milkshake to perform. Consider the competition. A bagel is hard to eat while driving. A sausage sandwich gets a steering wheel greasy. A banana gets eaten too quickly. It turns out that a milkshake is the perfect solution. Armed with this insight, an innovative fast food chain will look for other product ideas that solve the "boring commute" problem.[1]

The Customer's Job for Your Church

What "job" is your church's customer wanting you to do? That's an easy question, isn't it? Congregants attend a church to build social

---

1. Clayton Christensen, *The Innovator's Solution: Creating and Sustaining Successful Growth* (Boston: Harvard Business School Publishing Corporation), 76–77. Based on work by Anthony Ulwick.

capital, to get inspiration for life, to teach their kids how to live, to connect with God. The better you are at satisfying your customer's goals for these areas, the more successful you'll be.

There's just one problem with this: those people aren't your "customer"—God is. Remember the parable of the talents. Though the first two servants undoubtedly had customers to serve, their focus was on the pleasure of the master. *He* is the one they served. *His* are the goals that mattered. If a church is oriented toward faithfulness, it is oriented toward the problem *God* wants it to solve, the job *God* wants it to do.

As it turns out, this has everything to do with church operations. We often think about operations (administration, finance, personnel, technology, facilities, etc.) as the most "businesslike" element of the church budget. Yet taking this analogy too far can get us into a heap of trouble because God's job description for church operations is a world away from the job description for a business.

God's Job for Church Operations

What is God's job description for church operations? Let's look again at the administrative problem of Acts 6:1–7 to see how the apostles defined the job.

> In those days when the number of disciples was increasing, the Hellenistic Jews among them complained against the Hebraic Jews because their widows were being overlooked in the daily distribution of food. So the Twelve gathered all the disciples together and said, "It would not be right for us to neglect the ministry of the word of God in order to wait on tables. Brothers and sisters, choose seven men from among you who are known to be full of the Spirit and wisdom. We will turn this responsi-bility over to them and will give our attention to prayer and the ministry of the word."

This proposal pleased the whole group. They chose Stephen, a man full of faith and of the Holy Spirit; also Philip, Procorus, Nicanor, Timon, Parmenas, and Nicolas from Antioch, a convert to Judaism. They presented these men to the apostles, who prayed and laid their hands on them.

So the word of God spread. The number of disciples in Jerusalem increased rapidly, and a large number of priests became obedient to the faith.

Some context is helpful. As the first church expanded, it encountered a fault line of disunity along particularly troubling lines: the historical animosity between Greek-speaking Jews (Hellenists) and Aramaic-speaking Jews (Hebrews). Disunity in a church is a big deal since the mission of a church is to show off the glory of God, and disunity misrepresents God. Thus, Paul's rebuke to the divided Corinthian church was *theological*, not practical: their disunity lied about who Jesus is (1 Cor. 1:13). Beyond threatening unity, the administrative problem of Acts 6 also threatened the ministry of the Word: "It would not be right for us to neglect the ministry of the word of God in order to wait on tables" (Acts 6:2). Solving these problems was the job of this first church operations team.

A Mirror and a Messenger

To summarize, God's job for church operations in the first church was twofold. First, to support the church as a mirror of God's perfect, undivided character, and second, to support the church as a messenger of his perfect Word. The Jerusalem church was to represent God both in what could be seen and in what could be heard. In my experience, I've found strong parallels between this first church's challenges and our own: *operations exist to support the church as God's mirror and messenger.*

For the Jerusalem church, success is evident right there in these verses. Did they preserve unity? One intriguing detail in this account is that all seven deacons have Greek names. It seems that a majority Hebrew congregation bent over backward in the spirit of unity, entrusting their widows to deacons of the Hellenist minority. Why else would Luke allocate precious space to listing all seven names? Second, did they preserve the apostles' ability to preach God's Word? Note how verse seven summarizes the happy ending to this story: "the *word of God* spread" (Acts 6:7, emphasis mine). That's a job well done!

In a business, the *operations* aspect of the company aims at the bottom line: shareholder value. In a church, operations aim to support the church in its calling as mirror and messenger. In a business, getting things done matters more than how they get done (subject to ethical and legal limits, of course). In a church, *how* things get done—whether or not they preserve the church's ability to mirror the character of Christ—is an overriding concern. In a business, innovation is paramount; in a church, obedience is paramount. A business is mainly an enterprise—an organization geared toward doing something. A church is mainly a picture of Christ—an organization geared toward displaying something. This has multiple implications for operations in your church.

Operations Should Pursue Excellence

"Whatever you do, work at it with all your heart, as working for the Lord, not for human masters. . . . It is the Lord Christ you are serving" (Col. 3:23–24). This was true for the Colossian bond servant and it's true for those who labor in the church. How we execute even administrative tasks can say something about who God is. His excellence demands our excellence.

Too often, we excuse sloppy work in the church in the name of grace. We use staff positions as benevolence instead of hiring the best people possible. Volunteers and employees whose skills don't match the work at hand stay in their roles for years because we're afraid of

discouraging them. Grace, charity, and encouragement are critical to
the local church, but when abused they serve neither grace nor charity
nor encouragement.

That said, because our goal is faithfulness and not the bottom
line, excellence does not always imply efficiency. As a pastor, I often
let pastoral concerns trump efficiency—both in my shepherding and
my administrative work. But I must never pursue anything less than
excellence. In that sense, I'll define excellence as *using all your heart
and skill to do work that's worthy of the King with whatever time that's
appropriate*. The element of time constraints is important because
excellence doesn't always mean doing the best you can possibly do.
Instead, it means doing the best you can do with whatever time is
appropriate, given your need to be faithful in all areas of your life. For
example, excellence means giving the best of my skill and attention
to writing this chapter in the hours I've allotted to it. Excellence does
not mean neglecting my wife and children to make this chapter a
little bit better. "Do you see someone skilled in their work? They will
serve before kings; they will not serve before officials of low rank"
(Prov. 22:29). In all of life, we serve the King of Kings; let it show in
our work.

Operations Should Employ Deacon-Like Staff

A second implication of your church being both mirror and
messenger is that operational staff should view this mirror/messenger
calling as job one. You want operational staff who are like the Acts 6
deacons: people "full of the Spirit and wisdom" (v. 3). Hire those who
value efficiency and accuracy but hire those who value those qualities
as subservient to greater goals. You want staff who are willing to do
whatever it takes to keep the teachers of the church focused on teaching. You want staff who are willing to do whatever it takes to promote
the unity of the church.

Deacons have been described as the shock absorbers of the
church—they dampen any threats to unity that come their way.

We should look for operational staff with the same mind-set. That doesn't necessarily mean you build the diaconal qualifications of 1 Timothy 3 into the job description of your financial assistant. But whenever you hire someone at the administrative level, talk them through Acts 6 (job description for deacons) and 1 Timothy 3:8–13 (job qualifications for deacons). Explain how operations should support your church's roles as mirror and messenger—maybe even hand them a copy of this chapter.

Incidentally, this creates a strong argument for hiring members of your church. You're looking for those who will prioritize the unity and ministry of your church. Who better to do that than someone who has already committed to love your church? Aside from emerging legal reasons to restrict hiring to church members, the goals God has for operations in your church should give strong preference to hiring church members.

Operations Should Free the Congregation for Ministry

Then there's a third implication: operations should value ministry by the congregation. In Acts 6, deacons pursued administrative excellence in part to protect the apostles' Word ministry. Though not in view in Acts 6, we might apply the same principle to the *congregation's* Word ministry. After all, part of the ministry the congregation is equipped to do (Eph. 4:12) is "speaking the truth in love" (Eph. 4:15). Church operations should protect the pastors' teaching ministry; it should also protect the congregation's ministry that flows from that teaching.

What does this mean at a practical level? Design the operations section of your church's budget keeping in mind not merely financial stewardship but also the stewardship of your congregation's time and abilities. Would it be good financial stewardship for volunteers to clean the building each Saturday? Certainly. But balancing the priorities of time and money, would it be better stewardship to pay a contractor to clean so those church members could use the time instead to serve their neighbors, love their families, and encourage each other? That depends on the relative scarcity of time and money. But for many churches, the answer is yes.

Look for opportunities to free up your congregation from administrative ministry in order to engage in people-focused ministry. Administrative ministry is certainly honoring to God, and volunteers will always do much of it. But it is not always the best stewardship of those volunteer hours.

Operations Should Serve Ministry

Implication number four: avoid the temptation to let operations define constraints on ministry rather than the other way around. "No: we don't have money to do that." "No: we don't have space to do that." "No: that would never work with our schedule." Sometimes it's inevitable that operations will constrain ministry. But the job of church operations is to do whatever it takes so that ministry priorities can dictate direction.

I like to use battlefield engineers as a good analogy. The general decides to march his army fifteen miles to the east. The engineers perform whatever technical acrobatics are necessary to make that order a reality. Overnight, they build bridges, drain swamps, clear airfields—whatever it takes. In fact, if they're successful, the rest of the army might be forgiven for forgetting the engineers even exist. The excellence of their work removes operational limitations from the general's strategic planning.

Practically, how can operations wrongly control ministry? Avoid these operational responses whenever possible:

- *Answering no.* No one wants deacons or staff who constantly say no to new ministry ideas. They may not always be able to answer with an unqualified yes—but they might consider alternatives to a flat-out no. "Yes, we can do that—but help me decide which of these three things we'll need to stop doing to make it happen." "Yes, but that'll be a decision we need to bring to the whole congregation." "Yes, but do you have an idea of which budget item we could defund to get the money?" "Yes, I'm pretty sure we can do that, but let me take a week to get back to you with my best plan as to how it can happen." See how often those focused on operations can begin their answer with yes.

- *Acquiescing to financial constraints.* How tragic when the only thing blocking a good idea is a lack of money! Within reason, begin your planning without regard for budgetary constraints—and then figure out where to get the money. In my own experience, I've discovered that when lack of money is the only reason to give up on a new idea, there's almost always some way around the financial obstacle. In other words, don't give up easily when an idea looks good in every respect except for the financials. Remember, our God is unencumbered by financial constraints: "For every animal of the forest is mine, and the cattle on a thousand hills" (Ps. 50:10).

- *Establishing policies to avoid difficult conversations.* Have you ever heard this? "We need to establish a policy so that we never have to deal with *that* again." Policies *can* be beneficial to a church when based on solid principles. Many policies, however, are a broad-brush attempt to prevent the repeat of a difficult situation or avoid a difficult conversation. For example: a volunteer gets a speeding ticket driving the church van. In response, the church enacts a policy—the van may only be driven by church staff. Instead, you should simply ask *that* individual not to drive the van again, or to stick to the speed limit in the future. Over time, the accretion of reactive policies can put operations in the driver's seat instead of ministry, the proverbial tail wagging the dog.

Implications for Facilities

Everything I've said so far applies to operations and administration generally, including your church facility. But there are a few additional, building-related implications we should consider. Let's start with the purpose of your facility.

A Meeting Space, Not a Temple

Your building is *merely* a means to ministry; it is not sacred. To understand why, let me briefly take you through how Scripture describes sacred places. In the Bible, places *are* sometimes sacred. In Genesis 1 and 2, God created a sacred place, which he then filled with his sacred people (Adam and Eve). He later gave a sacred place, Canaan, to Abraham to be the home of a new sacred people. As his sacred people, Israel, entered that land, he gave them a new sacred place—the tabernacle—where he as holy God could dwell among his sinful (though sacred) people. Solomon replaced the tabernacle with the Temple; Nebuchadnezzar destroyed it.

Then Jesus arrived as the new Temple (John 2:19–21), the new meeting place of humanity with God. And Jesus inaugurated a new sacred people—the church. But where is the sacred place now? The temple is no longer a place but a people (1 Cor. 3:16). And we are waiting for our sacred place, the sacred city, the new Jerusalem (Rev. 21:2). In the old covenant, God created a sacred place and filled it with his sacred people. In the new covenant, God has created his sacred people, who are waiting for their sacred place.

Your church building, then, is neither tabernacle nor temple nor sanctuary nor sacred. It is simply a temporary meeting place for the people of God. That means its significance is not intrinsic to itself but only in the ministry it facilitates. As a result, the design of your facility should be centered on your church's calling as a mirror, imaging the unity of God, and as a messenger, holding forth the Word of God.

Let's take a closer look to see what that might mean for your building. My hope is that this next section is useful for you if you are building a new facility or looking to purchase a facility—or to help shape your long-term renovation plan if you're already in a building. In all, you'll want to answer the question: How can the facility our budget pays for better assist our faithfulness as a church?

Unity-Oriented

Let's look first at how a building can support church unity. What happens when people leave your weekly church service? Youth run away to the gym. Young adults head to the coffee shop. Parents grab their kids from the children's wing and make a beeline to the parking lot. Older folks head downstairs for their cherished potluck dinner. Is your building configured to divide or to unite?

My own church's building is more than one hundred years old and in the center of Washington, DC. It is crowded on Sunday mornings, without nearly enough space to accommodate those who want to spend time together after the service. Since the church was built in a historic district and doesn't have many options for expansion, I suppose there's not much we can do. But I long for a building that would better facilitate the unity of our congregation. As you have opportunity, create a facility that's oriented in that direction. That might include extra-large hallways and foyers where people can gather, lounge-type space for private conversations, or a main meeting room that feels more like conversation space (for after the service) than performance space.

The limitations of my building notwithstanding, its very existence has done much to encourage unity in the congregation. Its location creates a natural focal point for congregational life: half our members live within walking distance of the building. The generosity of those long-departed saints who built our building has given us a geographic "centeredness" that's done more for congregational unity than even the best fellowship space we could build.

Word-Oriented

The Protestant Reformation of the sixteenth and seventeenth centuries affected nearly every aspect of life, including church design. Out went church designs centered on an altar. In were church designs centered on a pulpit. Out went open floor plans, great for squeezing as many people as possible into a short mass. In were pews and balconies, perfect for getting the whole church together for a Word-centered sermon. In similar fashion, today's trends in church architecture reflect spiritual priorities.

As you think about dedicating funds to the design and creation of meeting space, consider creating space that is optimized for hearing the preached Word of God. In addition, consider the value of a space where the congregation can see and hear one another. In his teaching on corporate worship, Paul emphasizes not merely the worship of God but the edification of the church (1 Cor. 14:12; Eph. 5:19). The "audience" for corporate worship is the congregation as much as it is God. Accordingly, your space can reflect that, for example, in your seating configuration and in your lighting.

Finally, consider how you might create space that facilitates a Word-oriented schedule. For example, having multiple services because of space constraints designs congregational life around your facility, not the priorities of God's Word. I know this may sound crazy, but indulge me for just a paragraph.

A church schedule that's dictated by the facility seems backward to me. "We run three services on a Sunday, which means the service can't be more than sixty minutes, which means the sermon can't be more than twenty-five minutes" . . . and so forth. What an odd way to structure the most central aspect of a Word-centered church! Yes, I understand a facility sized to accommodate the whole congregation is expensive. Yes, I understand that people want multiple options in service times. And yet I'm convinced that we give up far more than we realize when we move to multiple services, which is why our Protestant forbearers would have been appalled to see our "mass-like" (in their opinion) multiservice church schedules. In our society, convenience trumps all; let's not make it so in the church.

HOW SHOULD A CHURCH
THINK ABOUT DEBT?

Given how often church facilities are financed by debt, it's useful to consider church debt in this section. Can debt play a legitimate role in a church's finances? Here are some questions to answer:

- Does your church's decision to go into debt wrongly influence how your congregants think about debt? Consider the standard of 1 Cor. 10:23: is this action "beneficial" to your congregation?
- What are your options for unwinding the obligation of debt if the future differs from what you anticipate? The borrower is slave to the lender (Prov. 22:7). This slavery can feel relatively benign if you are able to make payments as planned. Problems arise, however, when your circumstances change unexpectedly (Prov. 27:1). As a result, a church (or an individual, for that matter) should never enter into debt without knowing what will be required to get out of that obligation should circumstances change.
- What would be the negative impact on your faithfulness as a congregation if you save up to make this purchase instead of borrowing?

When you decide to take on debt, consider the following guidelines:

- Consider how far ahead into the future you can anticipate your circumstances when you set the term of your debt.

If your pastor is going to retire in five years, it is unwise to take on a twenty-year loan if you feel that departure may leave you with a diminished congregation.

- In determining your debt-to-equity ratio, be more conservative for ministry-critical assets (such as a meeting place) than for optional assets (like a home for your pastor).
- Speak about debt in a way that teaches your congregation how to think responsibly about debt.

Invest in Your Building

As you read this, do you see the priorities of the Word and unity reflected in your own church facility? Praise God! Many have advocated for a buildingless future for the Christian church, but when Christians have had the opportunity, they've nearly always invested in buildings. A church building gives stability to your weekly gathering. It provides a geographic focal point for the congregation. It facilitates midweek meetings. It can serve as the incubator for new churches. So don't be afraid to spend money on it.

How should you determine what money you need to spend on your facility? Consider dividing your facility spending into four different categories: major equipment maintenance and replacement (heating and air conditioning, sound, etc.); facility maintenance (light bulbs, toilet paper, etc.); facility repair; and facility renovation. When money for categories of infrequent spending (e.g., renovation) isn't comingled with ongoing expenses (e.g., maintenance), it can be easier to determine how much to set aside.

You'll see some suggested guidelines in the inset below to help you calculate how much you expect to spend per year in each category to keep up the facility. If you can't afford that calculated total, at least you'll have an idea of how far you're falling short. You might make up for this with unexpected income (say, the bequest of a departed member), a slower renovation schedule, or expectations of financial growth in the future. The difference between the facilities need you calculate and your actual facilities spending is your annual deferred maintenance, something that will be good to track over time.

HOW MUCH SHOULD WE BUDGET FOR FACILITY UPKEEP?

- Major equipment: calculate replacement cost divided by expected lifetime. You might escrow this money each year so that it is available when you need it.
- Facility maintenance and facility repair: a good starting point is average annual spending over the last several years.
- Facility renovation: ask a contractor you trust to give you an estimated renovation cost for your entire building. They might provide that figure as a cost per square foot or, with some additional work, a cost to renovate your entire facility. Divide that by how frequently you expect the church to need renovation on average (say, twenty, thirty, or forty years). That's your target renovation budget per year. As with major equipment, you might put budgeted money into escrow so that you add to your savings in years when you don't spend it on renovations.

What If We Don't Have a Facility?

Of course, your church may not own a building. That could be because you live in a place where churches can't meet legally; it could be because your congregation would like a building but hasn't yet been able to purchase one. Or it could be that you are in such a high-cost area that owning a building seems cost prohibitive. Your church will do just fine without a building. But let me leave you with three pieces of advice for your situation:

- Can you own or lease office space, even if it's not large enough to accommodate your whole church? In that space, you could do pastoral counseling, host small groups, provide midweek seminars, and more.
- If that's not an option, can you "adopt" a common midweek meeting space? Perhaps your pastor always works from one particular coffee shop so people know where to find him. Or your staff always have their staff meetings in one particular business incubator. The predictability of always using the same place for midweek meetings helps you develop a presence in the community and facilitates meetings among your congregation during the week.
- Can you recapture an old church building for the gospel? If you're in a city like mine, there are dozens of old church buildings with shrunken congregations. Sometimes a foresighted congregation is willing to give their building away to a newer, growing congregation—though that is unusual. But what if your congregation gives themselves away instead? Rather than thinking about these opportunities as "acquisitions," think of them as "revitalizations." Use your resources to help that church thrive—with their history, their congregation, and their identity. You may contribute money, leadership, and membership—but your focus is on bringing them back to life. It's a slower path than a building acquisition, but one that an older church might be more open to. And consider how revitalization benefits their Christian witness in the community. Instead of seeing the old church shut down to be replaced by a new one, they see the old church come to life!

Conclusion: Budgeting Is Pastoral

In a church, even budgeting for administration and facilities is pastoral in nature. Rather than aiming for pure efficiency, we should manage this section of the budget to help our congregations become better mirrors of God's character and better messengers of God's gospel. In fact, pastoral considerations pervade all aspects of church money matters. As such, the next chapter of this book is about communication: how to pastor your congregation through these many conversations.

CHAPTER EIGHT

COMMUNICATION

Using the Budget as
a Pastoral Tool

I n a detective story, the piece of the puzzle that *doesn't* fit is often
what solves the case. That's also true for the New Testament's teaching about money and the church—and that missing piece can shape
how you teach your church about money.

The New Testament Money Mystery

As is often noted, Jesus talked a lot about money. By some accounting,
he taught more about money than about heaven and hell. We might
expect that as the New Testament transitions to the Epistles' instruc-
tions to Christians, we would see the letters filled with "thou shalt give
to thy local church" commands. But we don't.

Yes, we see Paul telling the Galatians to support the teaching
they receive (Gal. 6:6). But that's it! That's all we've got to go on. Yet
clearly those early Christians were giving money to their churches
because the Epistles give plenty of guidance as to how churches might
spend their money. They were to support their preaching pastors
(1 Tim. 5:17). They were to support traveling missionaries (examples
in Rom. 16:1; 1 Cor. 16:11). The churches in Macedonia (Phil. 4:15)
funded Paul's missionary journeys. We see the *result* of congregations

giving (supported pastors and missionaries) without much instruction to do so.

The Didache, a first-century[1] manual of church organization, also indicates that giving was a regular part of life for early generations of Christians: "Take all the first fruits of vintage and harvest, and of cattle and sheep, and give these first fruits to the [teachers]. For they are your high priests. If, however, you have no [teacher], give then to the poor."[2]

In addition, we see commands about the spiritual priority of generosity (Rom. 12:8; 2 Cor. 9:11; 1 Tim. 6:18; 1 John 3:17), though exactly what that generosity funded seems to be of secondary importance. When Paul raised money for starving Christians in Judea, his overwhelming emphasis was on why we should give, not the need at hand (2 Cor. 8–9). In fact, except for his reference to the "poor" in Judea in Romans 15:26 and his mention of their "needs" in 2 Corinthians 8:14 and 9:12, Scripture tells us hardly anything at all about the need that motivated this ambitious project. Paul's focus was on spiritual good, not financial need.

So we see direction to churches on what to do with the money given to them by Christians, we see the result of Christians giving, and we see instruction to Christians to be generous with their giving. But no "thou shalt give to your church" command. Why? Presumably because the New Testament authors were far more interested in the spiritual well-being of these Christians than any particular financial needs. Paul's thank-you letter to the Philippians summarizes this emphasis: "Not that I desire your gifts; what I desire is that more be credited to your account" (Phil. 4:17). So, too, does his focus on being a *cheerful* giver (2 Cor. 9:7, emphasis mine). *The New Testament epistles care about giving not mainly as a means for meeting financial needs but as an indicator of what we love and whom we trust.* Which, of course, is very much how Jesus treated the topic.

---

1. Most scholars date the Didache to the first century. Some date it to the early second century AD.

2. *Didache* 13 [LCC 1, 177 f.]. What I've quoted as "teachers" is best translated as "prophets," though it's clear from surrounding context that the author is using that term as synonymous with "teachers."

All this carries significant implications for how you talk with your church about money. Your congregation's use of money matters mainly as a window into the well-being of their souls. That makes the budget more significant as a pastoral tool than a financial tool. It's more about the communication of eternal values than about balancing the numbers.

The Spiritual Values You Can Teach with Your Budget

This means that when you talk with your congregation about your church budget, consider teaching them things that are larger than the budget. Stop seeing the budget as a financial tool and start seeing it as a pastoral tool.

As you present the budget each year, *teach about the priority of faithfulness.* Your congregation's job is not to "lend God a hand" (as if his purposes are helplessly on hold until they cough up some money). Instead, their goal is to be counted as faithful. God is going to provide for every need he determines they have—he's promised that. Your church's budget simply represents a plan to be faithful should God provide as you expect.

When addressing funding shortfalls, *teach about trusting God-ordained constraints.* How do you react when your church can't fund everything you'd hoped it would? A right response: to be aggressive in faithfulness yet content with our limitations. Because the Lord is your portion, you can *always* say with the psalmist, "The boundary lines have fallen for me in pleasant places; surely I have a delightful inheritance" (Ps. 16:6).

When encouraging people to contribute toward the budget, *teach why they should give.* As Paul does in Philippians 4:17, we encourage people to give because it's good for *them* to give, not because God needs their gifts. We don't give to earn points with God or to avoid his discipline. We don't give out of guilt or fear but with joy, as we eagerly exchange what is passing away for what is eternal.

TEACH WHENEVER YOU TALK
ABOUT THE BUDGET

My church has six members' meetings each year; here are the topics I try to address in four to five minutes when I give a budget update.

- January: *The budget as a spiritual mutual fund.* Church leaders look for the very best spiritual investment opportunities and bring them to you in the form of our budget.
- March: *Why we give.* We give because it's good for us. Our "cheer" as givers (2 Cor. 9:7) shows that we value God and his plans more than we value the things of this world.
- May: *Why we have a budget.* For the Christian, giving should be thoughtful and deliberate, not a spontaneous response to an appeal. The same is true for our church; the budget helps us to be deliberate about where we invest.
- July: *Investing for faithfulness.* God doesn't need the money in our budget; he's doing just fine. But by being faithful with the money he's given us, we show off how good and trustworthy he is. Relatively speaking, we care very little whether or not we meet budget; what we're aiming for is to be counted as faithful.
- September: *Outreach spending.* Our goal for outreach spending is to help healthy churches start and grow both locally and around the world. Our goal for "in-reach" spending is to fuel the engine of ministry here in our own church.

> • November: *Love people more than the budget*. We take steps to make it clear that we love our people more than we love our budget (our reserve fund, deferring some building-related projects until a budget year has finished, etc.).

When making changes to the budget, *teach about good uses of money*. On the Last Day, we will see that some gifts to Christian charities produced tremendous fruit; some were just investing in false promises. When you add a new item to the budget, you can explain why it is a wise eternal investment. For example, "It's common to pull support from missionaries when they come off the field to get theological training, but we want to double down on Joshua's support while he's in seminary. It's wise to invest in theological discernment; it will help him do work that will last." Deleting an item from the budget is another opportunity to teach about priorities and values.

When adding staff members or positions, *teach about why staff exist*. Staff exist to equip the congregation to do ministry, not to do ministry on behalf of the congregation.

With all that said, let's look at two scenarios and see how you can use the budget to teach about God's economy.

What to Teach When Finances Are Ahead of Budget

You're midway through the year, and your church's income is 10 percent ahead of what you budgeted. Good news! And concerning, right? What if your people decide you don't need their money anymore? Will your church's good financial position dampen their faithfulness in giving? Here are a few things to talk about when your budget is ahead.

Ahead Doesn't Equal Success

I've often told my congregation something like this: "Much more than I care about how our budget is doing, I care about whether you're being faithful in your giving. I'm thrilled that we're ahead of budget. But if we're not being faithful in our giving, that's failure, not success."

We Need More Investment Opportunities

Investment managers sometimes "close out" a successful mutual fund. That is, they stop accepting new investors because they're concerned they might end up with too much money and run out of quality investment opportunities. I've never heard of a church doing that! Yet if you're not going to "close out" the budget, you're accepting a mandate to find high-value opportunities to invest in God's kingdom for every bit of money that your church receives. Being ahead of budget doesn't mean the hard work stops; it means the hard work begins as you seek new ways to invest that money.

What to Teach When Finances Are behind Budget

As challenging as it is to fall short of expectations, it's times like these that often prove most useful for teaching your congregation. Here's what to talk about when your church is behind budget.

Behind Doesn't Equal Failure

The budget wasn't revealed from heaven; it was merely your church's best guess as to what God would entrust you with this year. If you guessed wrong, that doesn't necessarily mean you've been faithless—but it's an important opportunity to examine how your church members are stewarding God's money. What matters most is faithfulness, not performance against the church budget.

God Will Provide What We Really Need

Giving that's 10 percent below budget simply means that our plan was 10 percent overextended.[3] All that God does is right, and never once in the history of the world has he given anyone an unfunded mandate. As Augustine prayed, "grant what you command, and command what you will."[4] God *always* gives what he commands.

Emergency Appeals for Money: Dangerous but Sometimes Prudent

One question we all face when the budget is behind is how we should explain the situation to the congregation. Do we simply provide the facts of the situation? Make emotionally-charged appeals for help? Somewhere in between?

This is a delicate matter. If you make a special appeal every year (or even every third or fourth year), you become the proverbial "boy who cried wolf." Beyond that, those most likely to respond are probably your most faithful members. And you run the risk of doing real spiritual damage by plaguing the congregation with false guilt for falling behind the budget. Perhaps fault lies not with them but with you, for drafting an unrealistic budget.

So how do you go about making such an appeal?

- *Rarely.* Take reasonable measures to avoid making such an appeal. For my own (relatively stable) congregation, I would like to avoid doing this any more frequently than once a decade. Keep in mind the ideas I gave you at the end of chapter three to avoid a situation where you "need" to make budget.
- *Because of temporary cash flow problems.* Before you make an appeal, you must be confident that the shortage is temporary,

---

3. Or, for the mathematically precise, $1/9$ overextended.
4. Augustine, *The Confessions of Saint Augustine*, book X, chapter 29.

not permanent. If a budget problem is likely to persist, the solution must begin with significant cuts to the budget. Be prepared to explain to your congregation the factors that make this shortfall temporary. Otherwise, they'll have little confidence you won't simply be making the same appeal next year.

- *For financial, not pastoral reasons.* This may seem counterintuitive given the tenor of this book. But special appeals are very limited in their pastoral utility. If your members are not giving faithfully, a special appeal is not the answer; teaching and prayer for faithfulness is the answer. A special appeal for help should be made simply because you want to avoid making long-lasting budget cuts to address what you believe to be a temporary problem. For example, perhaps you are in danger of having to lay off staff because of an economic slowdown in your area. If you have every reason to believe that income will pick up again in a year or two, it would be unfortunate to lose long-term staff because of short-term constraints.

- *Assume your members are giving faithfully.* Special appeals for money are often worded as to assume that most people aren't giving faithfully. For example: "If each of you would skip one latte each week for the next year, we could close our budget gap!" But embedded in that language is the assumption that Christians in your church will *normally* use their finances in selfish ways and that faithfulness is *ab*normal. Even if you have doubts about your flock's faithfulness, do not normalize faithlessness. An appropriate appeal is not, "I know you're all spending money on stuff you don't need; please give it to the church instead" but "this is the year to give in ways that you won't likely be able to repeat year after year." Communicate an expectation that healthy Christians will be faithful with their money.

A Note on Capital Campaigns

This advice also pertains to another kind of one-time appeal that churches make: capital campaigns. Perhaps you're looking to raise money for a new building or to retire debt or some other one-time expense. For many churches, a capital campaign can be a great service to its congregation.

But as you design your campaign, take careful note of the assumption that undergirds every capital campaign: that members have extra money lying around. If your campaign communicates, "Of course we all have money lying around that we don't really need," then it does a poor job of teaching your congregation what it means to follow Jesus.[5] More than the specific project at hand, the goal of a capital campaign is to highlight a kingdom investment opportunity that's uniquely tailored to one-time gifts.

Conclusion: More Blessed to Give Than to Receive

As Paul concludes his emotional farewell to the Ephesian elders in Acts 20, he calls to mind a saying of Jesus not recorded in the gospels: "It is more blessed to give than to receive" (v. 35). How amazing! Paul served the church at Ephesus "with tears" and "severe testing" (v. 19), yet he summarizes that as a blessing! To be sure, it *is* more blessed to give than to receive—more blessed to give our money, our time, our energy, our encouragement.

My prayer is that your church budget—how you talk about it, how you give to it, how you use it—is evidence to the truth of Jesus's statement. May we all live this life as if it is more blessed to give than to receive.

---

5. Sometimes wise and godly people end up with extra money that fits well with the goals of a capital campaign. For example, someone may have saved for retirement assuming the markets would appreciate at 5 percent per year while they performed at 7 percent instead. Or someone hoarded money as a non-Christian, got saved, and now wants to use what they'd hoarded for the Lord. Be careful to explain your capital campaign in terms that don't normalize faithless living.

NEXT STEPS

I began this book with Jesus's parable of the talents, where Jesus explains that the kingdom of heaven "will be like a man going on a journey, who called his servants and entrusted his wealth to them" (Matt. 25:14). Across these pages, we've looked at how a church's stewardship of its money can show off the goodness and glory of the master, with wide-ranging impact on a church's life together.

What Are You Going to Do Next?

In this concluding chapter, I'd like to talk with you about another stewardship, albeit a much smaller stewardship—the stewardship you now bear having read this book. Assuming you found a few nuggets of insight, you must determine how you'll steward that knowledge.

To that end, I submit for your consideration the following checklist of next steps that I've pulled from the chapters of this book. Read them through (and perhaps review the pages they came from if they seem unfamiliar) and check off which you want to pursue. Next steps might inform a conversation with your pastor, a memo for your elder board, a note of sermon application to file away, a question to pray through over the next week, a passage of Scripture to study in more depth—only you can determine the best next steps.

BUDGETING CHECKLIST

You can download an editable copy of this checklist
at https://www.9marks.org/budgetresources.

Chapter 1: Why Does God Care about Your Church Budget?

☐ Write out God's goals for your church budget (p. 31).

☐ Begin your next budget presentation with a brief over-view of Matthew 25 and the idea of faithfulness as risk-taking obedience (p. 26).

☐ Look at the section on how a faithfulness orientation changes a church's perspective on its budget ("What Difference Does Faithfulness Make?") and determine which of these six your church needs to consider most carefully (p. 31-33).

Chapter 2: Leadership

☐ Talk with your congregation about the church budget as a spiritual mutual fund (p. 35).

☐ Determine which of these three your church is weakest in: the pastors leading in administrative matters, the deacons supporting, or the congregation following (p. 38-41).

☐ Adjust the budget process so that your pastors lead it (p. 43).

☐ Look through the "Budget Tasks for Your Pastors" inset; which of these activities is (are) not being done by your pastors that should be their responsibility (p. 44)?

☐ Looking at the same list, for which of these activities should the pastors be looking for more help from the deacons and/or other individuals in the congregation (p. 44)?

☐ Are there any changes to your bylaws or accepted church practices that would be required for you to pursue any of your conclusions from the previous three items?

☐ Download and edit the online version of the Budget Discussion Worksheet (p. 50) so that it can be used in your church. https://www.9marks.org/budgetresources

Chapter 3: Income

☐ Have lunch to discuss this chapter with any members of your church leadership team who share Deacon Joe's mistaken "faith = a bigger budget" view of church finances (p. 54).

☐ Read "The Problematic Tithe" inset. Is there any way your church's teaching on tithing misleads your congregation about their responsibilities before God or his promises to them (p. 56)?

☐ Does your church wrongly emphasize spontaneity of giving versus Paul's advice in 1 Corinthians 16:2? If so, write out what you would like to do about that (p. 59).

☐ Talk with another church leader about better aligning your method for estimating income with the principles on pages 60–65.

☐ Which metrics described in the "Giving Metrics to Track" inset (p. 63) do you want to start tracking? Who should do this?

☐ Have a conversation among church leadership about things you do to help the congregation believe that their leaders love the congregation more than the budget. How can you do this better (p. 66)?

☐ Conduct short interviews of random church members or conduct an anonymous survey if you feel like your church is struggling with the previous item. Which changes to your process and/or communication could help remedy this problem?

Chapter 4: Staff

☐ Determine if your compensation team agrees with the four assumptions listed about 1 Timothy 5:17–18 (p. 72–73).

☐ Which of the staff hiring dos and don'ts are you most often in danger of violating (p. 76–77)?

☐ Have a person in an appropriate role interview each of the pastoral staff to determine if they feel their compensation leaves their ministry unhindered by financial need (p. 79).

☐ Determine which of the five compensation data points listed should be added to your compensation process (p. 80–81).

☐ See if your compensation committee can agree to all six of the items in the "Pastoral Pay Principles to Agree On" inset (p. 84).

☐ Ask your staff pastors if they feel that anyone else on the church leadership team is closely attuned to how well their compensation package is working (p. 83).

☐ As a pastor, are you misleading your congregation about how much money your family needs to minister effectively (p. 85)? If so, what are you going to do about that?

Chapter 5: Programs

☐ Have the following discussion with your leadership team: Of the programs and ministries in your church budget, which most appeal(s) to people as spiritual consumers (p. 91)? Are there any changes that should be made as a result?

☐ Another question to ask your leadership team: Which programs in the budget encourage similarity rather than diversity (p. 95)? How would you assess whether the benefits of those programs justify the degree to which they might hinder unity?

☐ How closely does your church's approach to funding programs and ministries approximate the "regulated, free-market" model (p. 97)? What would be the pros/cons of moving more in this direction?

☐ Use the "Ministry Assessment Worksheet" (p. 102) to evaluate the programs and ministries in your church budget as part of your next budget cycle. https://www.9marks.org/budgetresources

Chapter 6: Missions and Outreach

☐ Ask this question of your budget team: Does your current method of measuring effectiveness of outreach (missionaries, external ministries) acknowledge that real impact is at the discretion of the Holy Spirit (p. 105)?

☐ Look through the outreach section of the budget and mark any items that seem relatively unrelated to the Great Commission. What are you going to do about that?

☐ Rate each of your outreach investments for how well you know the work and how well you've structured those investments to increase your knowledge of that work going forward (p. 112–113).

☐ Put budget rules in place to protect outreach spending (p. 115).

☐ Determine what theological agreement an organization or missionary must share with you in order to be included in your outreach budget for the following categories: social ministry (e.g., combatting homelessness, pro-life advocacy), evangelism (e.g., student ministry), pastor training (e.g., seminary funding), church planting (p. 115).

☐ Set aside one day per week to pray through your outreach budget (p. 117).

☐ Download the "Missions/Outreach Scorecard" (p. 119) and use it as you begin to assemble next year's budget. https://www.9marks.org/budgetresources

Chapter 7: Operations

☐ Gather your administrative staff and teach them from Acts 6:1-7, showing them how their jobs support the church's role as a "mirror" and "messenger" (p. 123).

☐ In what area of administration and facilities is "excellence" as defined in chapter seven most lacking in your church (p. 125)?

☐ Look through the list of your administrative staff; are there any who do not seem to be deacon-like "unifiers" (p. 125)?

☐ Are operational constraints stifling any areas of ministry for your church (p. 127)? Can you think of anyone in your church who would have creative ideas for removing those constraints?

☐ Have a conversation among your church leadership team about whether your congregation's tendency is to undervalue or overvalue a church building (p. 133).

☐ If you're contemplating a building project, have the planning team read chapter seven, then discuss implications for project design.

Chapter 8: Communication

☐ Assemble a schedule of different teaching points to address whenever you present a financial update to the congregation, like the one shown in the "Teach Whenever You Talk" inset (p. 140).

☐ Flag the pages that describe what to teach when you are behind or ahead of budget and review it next time you're in that situation (p. 141–143).

☐ Have your leadership team read chapter eight and write down the positive and negative effects of special appeals for giving and capital campaigns on your congregation's faithfulness in giving. Then talk about whether you need to adjust your approach to these appeals.

The Joy of Stewardship

Stewardship is serious responsibility, both for us and our churches. As Jesus said, "From everyone who has been given much, much will be demanded" (Luke 12:48).

Yet it's also a joy, isn't it? If you've been a Christian for some time, consider how much of your joy comes from your own growth in godliness and how much comes from the growth of those around you. I love getting into God's Word; I cherish good times of prayer. But at this stage in my life, much of the joy I have in Christ comes from seeing God bear fruit in the lives of those I'm investing my life in. Consider the apostle Paul's experience with the Thessalonians: "For now we really live, since you are standing firm in the Lord. How can we thank God enough for you in return for all the joy we have in the presence of our God because of you?" (1 Thess. 3:8–9) or John's words in 3 John 4, "I have no greater joy than to hear that my children are walking in the truth."

I hope this book has helped to increase the joy of stewardship for you. Just think of the good that has come as your church's budget has kept a pastor in place year after year, proclaiming the good news of Christ crucified and raised. What amazing portrait of God's grace has he fashioned in your congregation through the ministry of the church, supported by solid administration and faithful programs? Or think of one of the missionaries you've been privileged to support. Is there a new church that's begun? Or two, or twenty? If those churches can hold on to the gospel for another twenty years, can you imagine the good that might happen? Do you see how in all that, God's goodness is proclaimed in ways that are far more profound than would ever be possible through your life alone? That's the joy of stewardship!

It is the joy of our stewardship that shows off how good and desirable God is, how good and desirable the work is he calls us to, and how good and desirable are his plans for us. So let's grow in that joy and look forward to that day when we will hear those words, "Enter into the joy of your master" (Matt. 25:21 ESV).

APPENDIX A

Budget Processes

n the following pages are sample budget processes for a variety of churches, followed by a comparison table.

POINTING PEOPLE TO CHRIST

Weekly adult attendance: 120

Location: East Point, Georgia

Denominational affiliation: none

BUDGET PROCESS (5 MONTHS)

☐ Finance team asks volunteer ministry leads to submit budget requests   Aug

☐ Finance team creates first draft of budget   Oct

☐ One staff elder and one lay elder review draft budget to align it with elders' vision and priorities   Oct

☐ Budget presented to deacons for feedback   Nov

☐ Budget presented to congregation at a members' meeting   Dec

☐ Elders adopt final budget   Dec

☐ New budget year begins   Jan

The Church at BROOK HILLS

Weekly adult attendance: 2,800
Location: Birmingham, Alabama
Denominational affiliation: Southern Baptist

BUDGET PROCESS (2.5 MONTHS)

☐	Budget proposals due from Pastoral Staff Team	Sept
☐	Revisions with staff	Oct
☐	Revised drafts due	Oct
☐	Initial presentation to Stewardship Ministry Team	Oct
☐	Revisions and adjustments as needed	Oct/Nov
☐	Final approval from Stewardship Ministry Team	Nov
☐	Presentation to Administrative Elder Team	Nov
☐	Approval by Administrative Elder Team	Nov
☐	Affirmation by the elder council	Nov
☐	Presentation to church	Nov
☐	Opportunity for questions	2 weeks
☐	Affirmation from church	Dec

KEY PLAYERS IN BUDGET PROCESS

- Pastoral Staff Team: all pastors on staff at the church
- Stewardship Ministry Team: team of deacons, appointed by elders, who advise in the creation of the budget
- Administrative Elder Team: senior pastor, executive pastor, elder chairman, and other nonelders

Weekly adult attendance: 375

Location: Portland, Oregon

Denominational affiliation: Conservative Baptist

BUDGET PROCESS (6 MONTHS)

☐	Send questionnaires to global supported workers	Jan
☐	Form compensation elder subcommittee	Jan
☐	Form missions elder subcommittee	Jan
☐	Elders provide initial guidance; staff, deacons, ministry leaders begin work on budget requests	Jan
☐	Elder vision and priorities meeting (results in three main priorities for next budget year)	Feb
☐	First draft of budget requests to executive pastor	Feb
☐	Executive pastor reviews and finalizes requests	Mar
☐	Elders set income line for budget	Mar
☐	Executive pastor helps elders adjust budget requests to balance the budget	Mar
☐	Elders present budget to deacons, small group leaders, Sunday school leaders	Apr
☐	Elders present budget to congregation	May
☐	Open budget Q&As with elders	Jun
☐	Elders meet to discuss any needed adjustments	Jul
☐	Congregation votes on the budget	Jul

MCLEAN PRESBYTERIAN

Weekly adult attendance: 1,200

Location: McLean, Virginia

Denominational affiliation: Presbyterian (PCA)

BUDGET PROCESS (8 MONTHS)

☐ Senior pastor and chief of staff present vision to Ministry Support Committee — Nov

☐ Elders finalize program guidance — Jan

☐ Finance director provides budget worksheets and schedule to budget managers — Jan

☐ Chief of staff and finance director meet with budget managers to communicate guidance and prepare draft requests — Feb

☐ Stewardship Committee discusses draft requests with budget managers — 2 weeks

☐ Stewardship Committee estimates income — Feb

☐ First draft of budget reviewed by senior pastor and chief of staff — Mar

☐ Finance director presents budget to Stewardship Committee for review and revision — Mar

☐ Budget revisions completed by budget managers — Mar

☐ Second draft presented to Stewardship Committee — Apr

☐ Budget presented to deacons — Apr

☐ Budget recommended to elders — Apr

☐ Elders approve budget for presentation — May

☐ Budget presented to congregation — Jun

☐ Elders approve and adopt budget — Jun

Stewardship Committee: subset of the Diaconate plus representatives from the Board of Women

	East Point	Brook Hills	Hinson	McLean
Denomination	None	Southern Baptist	Conservative Baptist	Presbyterian (PCA)
Metro area	Atlanta	Birmingham	Portland	Washington, DC
Weekly attendance	120	2,800	375	1,200
Who guides the budget process?	Finance team	Executive pastor	Executive pastor	Chief of staff
Who drafts budget requests?	Ministry leads (volunteers)	Staff	Deacons and staff	Staff
Who approves the budget?	Elders	Stewardship Ministry Team, elders, congregation	Elders, congregation	Stewardship Committee, elders
Congregational involvement	Feedback	Approval	Approval	Feedback

APPENDIX B

Language for a church's bylaws on congregational adoption of the church budget.

I f your church has the entire congregation approve its budget, you might consider language like what follows for your bylaws or constitution. This language is from the constitution of Capitol Hill Baptist Church in Washington, DC.

> A budget shall be approved by the membership at a members' meeting not more than three months after the start of the fiscal year. Prior to this approval and subject to the elders' discretion, expenditures may continue at the prior year's level.
>
> Each year the elders, after consultation with the deacons, the deaconesses, and the membership, shall present to the church an itemized budget. This budget shall be presented for discussion at a regular or specially-called budget meeting and called up for a vote at the following members' meeting. Congregational approval shall proceed, without amendment, as a single vote on the budget in its entirety. No money shall be solicited by or on behalf of the church or any of its ministries without the approval of the elders.

APPENDIX C

Annual Questionnaire for Supported Workers

Personal Information

Name:
Email:
Phone:
Skype ID:
Address:
Date of Birth:
Spouse/Children's names and birthdates:

Please attach a recent digital photo of your family.

Supporting Agency Information

Name of home church in your country of origin:

Name of board or agency with which you serve:

Appointment date:

Number of years serving in your country:

Relationship with Our Church

What was your initial connection to our church and with whom do you now have contact?

Are there ways in which our members might be genuinely helpful to your work by visiting you on a short-term basis in the next year?

Are there specific ways in which our church could more helpfully partner with your work in the next year and beyond?

We would love to have a leader from our church visit you in the next year, to get to know your work better and to encourage you. Is there a time of the year that would work best for that? Is there a reason why such a visit might not be helpful?

Please list items that we might provide that would enhance your work and/or family life.

Financial Information

What are your current budgeted financial needs per month?

What percent of your monthly budget needs are pledged?

Where does your giving come from? Please fill in the chart below.

	Congregations	Individuals	Other
% of support from . . .			
# of entities			

Optional: name and contact information for five largest supporters. This will help us coordinate in case of emergency or a special project.

Work's Strategic Importance

Give a brief description of your present work: the people who benefit and the challenges you face.

Please give a brief assessment of your work's importance.

Have there been any significant changes in your work in the last year?

How do you envision your work changing over the next year? Five years?

Church Newsletter

If you would like us to feature your work in written communication, please provide the following—otherwise, please leave this blank.

Location description (not specific, e.g., a big city in East Asia):

Description of your work:

Fun fact about your family:

Prayer items for your family:

Brief description of how you became a Christian and an overseas worker:

SCRIPTURE INDEX